THE DIGESTED READ

VOLUME II

JOHN CRACE

guardianbooks

First published in 2006 by Guardian Books
Copyright © John Crace 2006

The right of John Crace to be identified as the author of this work
has been asserted by him in accordance with section 77 of the
Copyright, Designs and Patents Act, 1988

The Guardian is a trademark of the Guardian Media Group plc
and Guardian Newspapers Ltd

ISBN
0-85265-063-9
978-0-85265-063-9

Cover Illustration: Joe Berger
Cover Design: Two Associates
Text Design: www.carrstudio.co.uk
Printed and bound in Great Britain by
William Clowes Ltd, Beccles, Suffolk

10 9 8 7 6 5 4 3 2 1

Contents

Chick and lad lit

Sport

Sleaze

Beyond help

Middle of the road

Very important science and politics

Try-hards

9/11

Shock and awe

Eurotrash

North Americana

Oedipal reads

Introduction

If you have already bought the first volume of the Digested Read you can probably skip this bit and dive straight into the rest of the book. But those of you who are coming to it for the first time, or only started reading the column when it moved to the back page of the new g2, might like a bit of background.

The Digested Read has been a regular weekly feature in the *Guardian* for nearly seven years and I have been writing it for more than six and a half. My brief is to take the most talked-about new book of the week – anything from the latest offering from a Booker-prize-winning author to a TV celebrity's most recent autobiographical update – and retell the story in about 500 words in the style of the author.

No one and nothing is sacrosanct and as with any pastiche, the prime purpose is to entertain. But that's not the only aim. Read any film, theatre or music review and you'll notice that the critics don't hesitate to put the boot in when they feel it is deserved. But rarely will the literary critics give a book a total pasting.

You don't generally find Francis Ford Coppola reviewing the latest Coen brothers movie, but in the books pages you do find well-known writers reviewing each others' work. The attractions of playing safe are all too obvious: who wants to risk calling a turkey a turkey when it may be you that's next in the line of fire? Some people feel that my pastiches are a little on the harsh side and it is true that I have come to read books rather differently to most. Where others read to be dazzled, I read for clunky dialogue, pretentious stylistic tics and a complete absence of big ideas.

One of the biggest joys since the first volume was published has been the number of great authors who have contacted me to say how much they enjoy the Digested Read. I won't embarrass them by blowing their cover, but I am very touched to be on the end of a generosity of spirit that I weekly fail to reciprocate. On the other hand, it has also come to my attention that there are a group of die-hard authors who can't stand the Digested Read and hate its lack of reverence for the demi-gods of the written word. So, naturally enough, this book is dedicated to them.

John Crace, July 2006

The digested read...

Prizewinners and nominees

The Clerkenwell Tales

Peter Ackroyd

"There will be five fires and five deaths in London," shrieked Sister Clarice, the mad nun of Clerkenwell.

"Her prophecies are given credence by the people," said Sister Agnes. "Did you smell her fart?"

She serves my purpose well, thought Robert Baybroke, Bishop of London.

"Listen carefully," said William Exmewe, to the simpleton Hamo. "We are the predestined ones. All is foretold by providence. Five churches must be burnt."

"Forsooth, I need an arse-wipe," groaned Radulf Strago. "The Merchant's tale is almost over," smiled his wife.

"The Lollers will be blamed for the fire at St John's," Exmewe whispered. "Twas well done." Soon the second church would be ablaze and the Eighteen Conclusions nailed to the altar.

"The game is begun," said Miles Vavasour. "Your deception serves us well, Master Exmewe. The predestined ones have done our business and Dominus remains unknown. Soon Henry Bolingbroke will replace the leech King Richard."

"I am your father," cried Oswald Koo.

"Why are you here?" asked Sister Clarice.

"We needed a Reeve's tale."

"God's turds," said Thomas Gunter, "I must be the Physician's tale."

Bolingbroke was in England and the king's days were surely numbered. The smell of putrid faeces and rotting corpses wrought the air.

"The miller's daughter had a child out of wedlock to give us a Miller's tale," Sister Clarice said.

Exmewe withdrew his dagger and slit Hamo's throat. "My plans are compromised."

"The man has a counterfeit face," muttered Gunter as he followed Vavasour to Dame Alice, the procuratrix. "She must be the Wife of Bath."

"Why am I here?" Gybon asked the bishop.

"To fulfil the Squire's tale."

Richard was now in the tower and Henry at Westminster. Exmewe watched Vavasour depart. "The physic knows our secret. Both our days are numbered."

"God give you grace," said the Pardoner, his tale done.

"In the name of Dominus, I kill you," Exmewe laughed as he stabbed Gunter. "Had the Shipman seen us, we would have been in his tale."

John Ferrour was confessor to Henry. He looked at Vavasour. "Your penance is to journey to Jersualem, leaving all your possessions behind."

"So that was the Parson's tale," said Henry.

Sister Clarice uttered a final prophesy. "If an unhallowed king should come to rule then others must hold power for the anointed one."

"I have my tale," said the second nun, and within four months Richard was dead.

"I exile you, Exmewe, to France," said Baybroke. "Now we are safe. We are the holy ones. We will rule behind the king. Dominus rises."

The digested read ... digested

The stench of faeces rises in the Author's tale

Alentejo Blue

Monica Ali

"Gosh it's hot," Joao said to himself, vividly creating an image of the harsh, sunburnt Portuguese countryside. As he dragged his 84-year-old body out into the forest to relieve himself, he stumbled across his friend, Rui, hanging from a tree. "Change comes to us all," he thought deeply. "They even say that Marco Alfonso Rodrigues is coming back to Mamarrosa to build a hotel."

Stanton lounged with limpid languidness in Vasco's bar. Vasco and Eduardo were arguing about what would happen when Eduardo's cousin, Marco Alfonso Rodrigues, returned. Who cared? Stanton thought, as the Potts girl, Ruby, caught his eye. She was getting a bit of a reputation in the village.

* * *

Jay Potts interrupted Stanton's rural reverie. "Come over and visit us?" the young boy said. Stanton was too tired to argue. Ruby's mother, Chrissie, looked meaningfully into Stanton's darkly hooded eyelids. Stanton lifted her skirt and entered her roughly.

Their relationship ran out of steam as quickly as the chapter, but Stanton wasn't bothered. He had moved on to Ruby; or rather she had moved on to him. Sometimes it was hard to care.

Vasco's anus fizzed with tension. What would happen if Eduardo's internet cafe ever got internet access? And what would happen if Marco Alfonso Rodrigues arrived in Mamarrosa? If only his wife hadn't died so tragically.

My husband has a strange way of disagreeing with me. And I have a strange yet stylistically profound way of introducing a minor character in the first person. He'll say, "Come on, Eileen, you know

4

what I mean," when he doesn't. He's never come to terms with the fact that our son Richard is gay.

* * *

Teresa's mind was a cauldron of confusion. In a few days she would be working as an au pair in London. But how could she break the news to her mother? And what if her brother, Francisco, had got Ruby pregnant? First, though, she must lose her virginity to Antonio.

"Everything is ready," Antonio mumbled, his hard, hornery hand caressing her thigh. A knock on the door interrupted their embrace. It was Vicente and Paula. Vicente rolled a joint and slipped himself inside Teresa. Antonio could always be the second, Teresa thought with a cold, calculating detachment.

"I can't believe this is happening," said Chrissie, as her husband told her the police were going to charge her with the murder of Ruby's baby. "Well, it's not," the police replied. "Hospital records show the foetus died naturally after all." "Phew," said everyone.

Sophie and Huw drove excitedly into Mamarrosa. In a fortnight they were due to be married. "How excited I am to be getting married," gurgled Sophie. "Me, too," growled Huw. But as the Alentejan dust insinuated its way under their skin, so did the doubts. "Maybe we shouldn't get married after all," Sophie mewed. "Whoever can know for sure," said Huw.

A caped man strode into town. "It's Marco Alfonso Rodrigues," cried Eduardo. "Love and peace," Marco murmured. Stanton decided it was time to move on. Eileen thought Huw would be the perfect partner for Richard. Antonio and Vicente were fighting.

"Marco Alfonso Rodrigues has left," yelled Vasco, embracing Eduardo. "He must have been an impostor."

The digested read ... digested

Mad Portuguese and Englishmen go out in the midday sun

The Blind Assassin

Margaret Atwood

My sister, Laura, drove her car off a bridge in 1945. The police said
someone had seen her deliberately swerve; I told them it was an
accident. Out of respect for my husband, Richard, they believed
me. Who knows where to find the hurt?

The Blind Assassin by Laura Chase

She took off into the night to find him among the anonymous
apartments in the tenement district. He pulled her close. "We haven't
much time," he insisted. "Tell me a story," she replied. So he started
to tell her of the city of Sakiel-Norn, the sacrificial virgins and
the blind assassin. Laura has become a cult writer since her book
was published after her death. Scholars ask me for details. I give
them none. My parents married in 1914. She gave him class, he
gave her money. He was never the same after he came back to
Port Ticonderoga from the war. He drank too much, but was still
loyal to the men in his button factory. I was born in 1916, Laura
in 1920. My mother died after a miscarriage. That changed
everything.

My father had a bohemian friend, Callista, who came to give him
comfort. She once introduced us to Alex Thomas; he was a
revolutionary. He was later accused of bombing my father's factory,
but Laura and I hid him. Laura was fond of him. I expect you might
guess who the characters in Laura's book really are now.

The depression hit my father hard. "I think you should marry
Richard Griffen," he said. "Laura needs looking after." I didn't love

him but had no choice. Richard took me hard on our wedding night; he liked it like that. He never told me father had died till we got back from honeymoon. "Laura's unwell," he said. "I've put her in a sanatorium." I had lost her. I gave birth to Aimée; she didn't look anything like Richard. Can you guess the story now? Help me, because this is difficult.

Alex and I are the lovers in the book. I wrote it under Laura's name. I once thought that she and Alex were lovers, too. But their love was different. Her pain was not of Alex's making. She had regularly been abused by Richard.

You didn't leave your husband then. I did, and I paid for it. Aimée was taken away and I've lived in poverty since. I'm now an old woman. I don't ask for love or understanding. Just your time.

The digested read ... digested

The innocent but all-too-knowing Iris Chase trawls through her family history in a sort of prewar Aga saga

Millennium People

JG Ballard

My involvement began when I was due to fly to America. My wife, Sally, was struggling with the packing when the phone rang – she insisted on pretending to be crippled because she still had not come to terms with her accident.

"There's been a bomb at Heathrow," she said. I turned on the TV to see my ex-wife, Laura, lying in the wreckage.

"There's lots of these fringe groups," said Henry at the funeral. "Major Tulloch has asked me to investigate. But I don't think I will."

But I would. I started at a cat show at Olympia. Cats are more dangerous than they seem and in a tussle with the police I was arrested and fined £100. I found the experience curiously liberating and as I left the court a woman picked me up and drove me to Chelsea Marina.

"We middle classes are the new proletariat," Kay said. "We're all just scraping by. We need to shake people up." Kay introduced me to Richard and Stephen.

"We middle classes are the new proletariat," they both said.

"So Kay keeps telling me."

"Well, you're going to hear a lot more of it over the next 200 pages."

Shaking people up involved setting fire to a video shop and burning down the NFT. I felt anxious but alive.

"You're spending a lot of time away from home," said Sally, who was having an affair with Henry.

"I'm finding myself."

I was no nearer to finding out who had bombed Heathrow when

an explosion at the National Theatre killed three people.

"They're selling out," sighed Richard. "They'll settle for getting their maintenance charges reduced. They need to do something pointless."

"We middle classes are the new proletariat," said Kay in case it had slipped my mind during our vigorous love-making. "By the way, Stephen has gone missing."

"We need to find Stephen," said Richard. "He's just killed a TV personality in Fulham. I'm off to Hungerford."

"Aren't Jill Dando and Michael Ryan so last millennium?" I asked.

"Yes, but this is satire."

I found the car at Heathrow. "So it wasn't Stephen who bombed the airport or killed the TV personality?" I asked.

"It was me," Richard said. "I'm trying to be pointless."

Stephen shot Richard and placed the gun in my hand. "I'll take that," said Major Tulloch. I realised later that they had known about my involvement all along but wanted me to get close to the leaders. There was nothing the establishment feared more than a middle-class revolution.

With Richard's death and the end of service charges, the movement fizzled out. Kay became a TV presenter. I got back together with Sally. She even started walking. We found ourselves. My name's Ben Elton. Goodnight.

The digested read ... digested

Bourgeoisie of the world unite. You have nothing to lose but your Range Rovers

Arthur & George
Julian Barnes

Arthur

His father had a penchant for alcohol, and it was the mam who moulded him into the rumbustious lad he was to become. His time at Stonyhurst is not altogether unpleasant, though he did suffer nocturnal emissions.

George

George does well at the village school when moved to the front of the class. The oculist declines to give him glasses. His father, the vicar of Great Wyrley, says "Blessed are the meek" when boys make monkey faces at his son.

Arthur

Having been to sea, Arthur fulfils his duty by marrying Louise Hawkins, whom he calls Touie. He qualifies as an ophthalmic doctor but prefers to write; he is soon the bestselling author of Sherlock Holmes.

George

George regrets appearing alongside Arthur in a biography masquerading as fiction. The obsessive attention to detail reminds him of his own book on railway law. "I was hoping for something more emotionally engaging," he says to himself.

Arthur

Touie has been struck down by consumption, and Arthur has bought a house in Surrey, where the climate is more agreeable. He has two children and would never leave her, but he has been courting Jean for some time – platonically, apart from the time when he spontaneously soiled his underlinen.

George

A series of poison-pen letters has been sent to the vicarage. These stop in 1896 and George qualifies as a solicitor. But they start again in 1903, and Great Wyrley is beset by horse-ripping. Captain Upton blames the blackamoor. "I am arresting you, George Edalji," he says. "The Parsee pronunciation is Aydlji," George replies.

George

George is a model prisoner and is released after three years. He is surprised the book is three-quarters done and nothing has happened.

Arthur

Since Touie died, Arthur has been looking for a project. George's letter asking for help restoring his name is the very thing. George was clearly too myopic to have committed the crime. "You are a bounder, Captain Upton," he says. "You are prejudiced against George because he is coloured and because you think he is a homosexualist." He writes an article accusing George's former schoolfriends, which some compare to Zola's *J'Accuse*.

George

George is now moderately happy, but he fears Arthur has taken over his life.

Arthur

"Cads," he yells. "They've acquitted him of ripping but say he wrote the poison-pen letters to himself. George will come to my wedding to Jean."

George

It is 20 years on and George is grateful for his life. He attends a seance for Arthur at the Albert Hall and wonders if it's all a load of nonsense.

The digested read ... digested

The bland leading the blind

The Laying On of Hands

Alan Bennett

Anyone looking around the congregation and its celebrity assortment might have imagined that Clive had been a sociable creature. But the gathering owed more to Clive's discretion than his friendships, and many household names had been mildly irked on entering the church to discover they were not the sole centre of attention.

Clive had died in Peru and, when a young man dies in unknown circumstances of an unknown disease, the question, "What did he die of?" often assumes a personal dimension for those who remain. Father Geoffrey Joliffe, who was about to take the service, was no exception. By profession, Clive had been a masseur, but he had interpreted the word generously, and although Geoffrey had little reason for anxiety – his guilt had kept their encounters to minimal bodily contact – his confusion of God with Joan Crawford often was enough to inspire alarm.

As the service neared its conclusion, Father Joliffe had some regrets. Much had been spoken of Clive's charms, but nothing that he felt truly captured the essence of the Clive he had known.

"If anyone has any further reminiscences they would like to share, they are invited to do so now," he improvised.

Various people stood up to extend their thoughts, before Carl stepped forward. "I would like to tell you what Clive was like in bed," he began.

"I didn't know he was gay," chorused several women.

"And when someone that young dies of Aids, it's time for anger as well as grief," Carl continued.

The mention of the word that mustn't be mentioned caused a frisson.

"He didn't die of Aids," said a young man named Hopkins. "I was with him in Peru. He was bitten by an insect."

"They all say that," snarled Carl.

"I'm his doctor," ventured a smartly dressed man. "His latest blood test was negative."

As the congregation peeled away, their hearts were considerably lighter than when they entered. Hopkins approached Geoffrey. "I have Clive's diary," he said.

Seeing his initials against several dates, Geoffrey laid his hands on Hopkins' knees. "I'll take care of that," he whispered as Hopkins bolted for the door.

Some weeks later there was a knock on the vestry door. "I thought, why not?" said Hopkins.

The digested read ... digested

The Book of Revelations

The Bay of Angels

Anita Brookner

As a child I was minded to think that, as in fairy tales, hardships brought their reward, so I was content to accept my lot with passivity. My mother and I lived in distressed gentility in Edith Grove; my father had died when I was small, a source of puzzlement to me and regret to my mother, and we coexisted in proximity, if not closeness, as neither presumed to burden the other with the intensity of our profound emotions.

I was relieved when my mother met Simon. He was much older and held the assumptions of his generation, but he was kind and we could not have asked for more. He bought me a small flat, which gave me a modicum of independence, and my mother and he moved to his home in Nice. Away from the confinement of my mother, I entered a relationship with Adam, a far freer spirit than that to which I was accustomed. I might have been saddened, if not jealous, at his affairs with other women had I been otherwise minded, but I grew to value the times he chose to share with me.

Adam was not to Simon's tastes; our visit to Nice was far from a success. I used to hear Simon listening at our door to see if Adam had crept into my bed, which, being of a hotter temperament, he invariably had. It was with a sense of relief on all sides that we returned to London, and my relationship with my mother reverted to a formal normality.

It was with some shock that I heard Simon had fallen and died. My mother had been so overcome that she had been taken to hospital for a sleep cure. I moved to Nice, where it was with some annoyance that I found Simon had been financially incautious and I was forced into more straitened circumstances.

My conversations with Dr Balbi led me to believe my mother was unlikely to recover, but I was obliged to continue my visits. Dr Balbi encouraged me to think he desired me but, despite ten pages of intense introspection and repressed sexual longing followed by a raised eyebrow, he failed to make an advance.

Some months later I observed the formalities of my mother's death and found myself financially comfortable once more. Dr Balbi – dear Antoine – now spent the occasional night with me. We were not more open about our relationship for fear of upsetting his sister. One day I might even contemplate a life without him. How bold I have become.

The digested read ... digested

More intense feelings valiantly repressed and cruel suffering nobly borne as another Brookner heroine lies back and thinks of Chelsea and Nice

Theft: A Love Story

Peter Carey

This is a love story, though that did not begin until midway through the shitty stuff, by which time I had lost everything to my ex-wife, who is called the Plaintiff and definitely not Alison. When I got out of prison, I'd taken my simpleton 220lb brother, Hugh, to live with me in a house in New South Wales, which I'd been lent by my benefactor, John-Paul.

I'd started work on a new canvas, and Hugh was playing with his dead dog and breaking people's fingers in the local bar, when this woman turns up in a pair of Manolos and says, "I'm Marlene Liebovitz. Did you know your neighbour has a Joseph Liebovitz?"

PHTAA. We are the Bones. My BROTHER is called Michael Boone but everyone calls him Butcher Bones ON ACCOUNT of our dad being a butcher and one of the Os falling off the shop SIGN.

It's me, Butcher, again. Don't worry too much about Hugh's interruptions. Every writer who wants to be taken seriously has to introduce an experimental voice into the narrative. Detective Amberstreet accused me of stealing the Liebovitz and painting over it, and then walked off with one of my canvases. Back to Sydney, then, where I unrolled some paintings on the Plaintiff's lawn while Hugh farted. Jean-Paul offered me $10,000. If I knew then what I know now, I might have been grateful.

SCUTTLEBUT and SMELLS IN HELL. I had taken my CHAIR out on the street when MARLENE walks into the GALLERY. The CONVICTED CRIMINAL never knew I fancied her, but I could tell HE WAS GOING to shag her.

When I saw Marlene again I knew she had stolen the Liebovitz but I was swept away by a bottle of whisky. "I love your work," she purred. "I can get you an exhibition in Tokyo." If I knew then what I know now, I might have refused.

FORGIVE ME for interrupting, but the IDIOT SAVANT can be SAVANT. So if you want to know why BUTCHER always ends his chapters the SAME WAY, it's because he's been told IT'S a CREATIVE writing TECHNIQUE of injecting non-existent TENSION into the story.

"Look," said Marlene, "All your paintings have sold and I've found a Japanese buyer for my Liebovitz." She pulled me close, making me forget that she was still married to the artist's son, Olivier. Had I remembered I might not have gone to New York with her.

I haven't been doing MUCH for 50 PAGES, but now I'm FARTING ON A PLANE to America with Olivier.

Amberstreet followed us to New York but he still couldn't pin the theft on Marlene. "How did you fool him?" I asked. "It was mismeasured in the catalogue," she smiled. Life was no fun as an unknown artist so, God help me, I created a copy of one of Liebovitz's lost masterpieces. Marlene was furious when Olivier wanted a divorce. "How can we now authenticate the work?" she cried. Days later, Olivier turned up dead. I knew Marlene had done it even though she tried to blame Hugh by breaking a finger on the stiff. It was time to leave.

HEAD DOWN and ARSE TO THE BREEZE. TOUCH of CLASS.

Years have passed. My paintings sell for hundreds of thousands and the Liebovitz sold for millions. I haven't seen Marlene but I know it's her way of showing she loves me.

The digested read ... digested

GIVE me the Booker PRIZE again

On Green Dolphin Street

Sebastian Faulks

Charlie van der Linden looked at his empty Martini. His hands were still shaking. "Time for a Scotch." The last party of the 50s in DC was in full swing.

"Meet Frank Renzo," Charlie said to his wife, Mary. "He's a reporter from New York." Mary smiled and went upstairs to watch her children as they lay sleeping. "I really am the happiest woman in the world," she thought.

A few days later the phone rang. It was Frank. "I'm writing a feature on embassy life. I'd like to take you to lunch."

"I'll need to check," Mary countered.

"If ever you're in New York, I'd be happy to show you round," Frank announced casually over a coffee.

It had been the most amazing three days in Manhattan. "Check out Kind of Blue," smoothed Frank.

"Nice," Mary replied. She hesitated. "You are the most remarkable man."

"I love you, too," he answered as their lips met. "We mustn't," she sighed, pressing herself tighter to him.

"You're right," he groaned, cupping her breasts in his hands.

"Donchew worra bout me," slurred Charlie, as he washed down a fistful of barbiturates and Tylenol with a half-bottle of Scotch.

"I've got bad news," said Frank, pulling Mary close. "John Coltrane's split from Miles Davis. Oh, and I'm not going to be able to see you so often. I've been put on the Kennedy election campaign trail."

"I won't be able to see you for a while, either," she replied, her eyes moistening. "My mother's dying of cancer, and I must fly back to London to be with her."

At least the separation will give us plenty of pages to reflect on their angst.

"I'm being posted to Moscow to brief the embassy on the new president," said Charlie, his whole body trembling.

"Bad news, Mrs van der Linden," barked a Foreign Office official. "Your husband's had a breakdown. We need you to bring him back from Moscow."

"I love you so much, Charlie," Mary cried, as her husband came out of the psychiatric hospital.

"You'd better go back to Washington to close up the house," he replied.

"I love you so much, Frank, I'll stay in the US." This was even tougher than Guadalcanal. "I love you, too," he said. "But you must go back to London."

"I've changed my mind," he sobbed, as her plane flew overhead.

The digested read ... digested

Embassy wife and US hack develop their own special relationship, but choose not to come in from the cold

The Idea of Perfection

Kate Grenville

Harley Savage surveyed the stillness of Karakarook, NSW, population 1,374. It had been the offer of free accommodation that had nudged her from Sydney to this backwater to advise on the Heritage Museum. Go on, go.

"Is everything all right?" asked Coralie Henderson.

Don't let her see your dangerous streak. Don't mention the family.

"Fine," she replied, absentmindedly.

Douglas Cheeseman cursed himself as he drove out to the bent bridge. Why hadn't he brought his *Engineering Digest*? Sitting in silence made him feel so awkward. Ahead, he spotted a large, middle-aged woman walking in the heat.

"Good day," he said.

"Good day," she replied.

"Would you care to join me for tea tomorrow?" Why had he been so intimate, he wondered.

"OK."

Later, as he studied the bridge he was to demolish, Douglas wondered whether he should have offered her a lift.

As Harley returned home, she wondered whether she should have told the strange, jug-eared man that she had to walk for an hour each day due to her infarction. Why had she accepted his offer? Friends called her *jolie laide,* but she was neither *jolie* nor *laide.* Just plain. Why couldn't she have kept her distance and her dangerous streak hidden?

"I suffer from bad vertigo," said Douglas, over tea. "But I find concrete very interesting." To Harley's surprise, it was.

A day later, she got into difficulties swimming in the river. She couldn't drown. She couldn't leave Douglas with the guilt of being the last person to see her alive. The same guilt she felt about her third husband, who had committed suicide with a circular saw.

Douglas saw Harley among the bridge protesters. He felt a surge of anxiety. But was it his responsibility to tell his superiors there was another way of mending the bridge?

He awoke to the smell of burning. The butcher's shop next door was on fire and Harley's patchwork quilt was inside. Fighting his vertigo along the fire escape, he climbed inside to rescue it.

Lying on Harley's day bed, Douglas explained how the bridge could remain bent if the corbels were replaced with concrete. Things would not go wrong this time, Harley reflected. Harley, of the dangerous streak, had broken open.

The digested read ... digested

Two displaced middle-aged Aussies somehow fashion a bridge, a patchwork quilt, a relationship and the Orange prize

Notes on a Scandal

Zoë Heller

This is not a story about me. But as the task of telling it has fallen to me, it is right I should tell you a bit about myself. My name is Barbara Covett. It won't mean much to you, I'm sure, but you'll soon recognise my type. I am the unreliable narrator, the first resort for any hack who wants to be taken seriously as a novelist.

Sheba is upstairs sleeping, so now is a good time to continue. She doesn't know I am writing an account of last summer's events. But I think it will be valuable to document the hysterical prurience her actions unleashed.

I first met Sheba when she came to teach pottery at St George's. I recognised immediately that she was different to the rest of us – posher, more confident. I kept myself to myself at first. I'd taught at the school for umpteen years and seen many teachers come and go, and I must confess I had my doubts about her.

She later told me of her first meeting with the Year 11 boy, Connolly. "He tried to kiss me," she said. "You must tell the head," I cautioned. "Oh, no. It was just an innocent advance. It's over."

This turned out to be far from the truth, but it was not till some months later that Sheba confided in me that she and Connolly were having an affair. "It's so exciting," she said, "we're in love."

It struck me at the time that it was almost unbelievable for a 40-year-old woman to be so head over heels in love with a 15-year-old boy. But then it also struck me as unbelievable that she would have become such good friends with me, a dowdy working-class spinster. Still, it's only fiction after all.

"You must stop the affair," I urged. "You'll damage your family and your career. Think of your poor son with Down's syndrome whose purpose in life is to create moral dilemmas and engage the reader's sympathy."

Sheba promised she would end it, but her repeated absences suggested otherwise. I must own up here to some envy that she made so little time available for me, and when Brian Bangs, the staff-room Lothario, told me he had a crush on her, I couldn't resist intimating my knowledge of the affair.

"I think Bangs knows," I later warned her, but by then events were out of control. Connolly, I gather, had tired of the affair, but his withdrawal only spurred Sheba to greater follies. She began taking risks and before long Connolly's mother found out and accused her of sexually abusing her child.

Sheba had to leave the school, of course, as did I. Her marriage ended and we now share a house. She is coming downstairs.

"I've found your notes," she yells. "It didn't happen like that at all. I'm leaving."

But she can't. There's no place else for her to go.

The digested read ... digested

Unbelievable love triangle between the posh, the old and the spotty

English Passengers

Matthew Kneale

"That bleb Quayle," muttered Captain Kewley of the *Sincerity* to his Manx crew. "If he hadn't have kept the cheese we'd have fooled that sleetch Clarke. Now, we've got to pay a £200 fine. Where will we get the jink?"

"I can prove the atheisms of geology," exclaimed the Rev Geoffrey Wilson. "Having studied the Bible, I am certain the Garden of Eden is to be found in Van Diemen's Land."

"I am bound there myself," replied Dr Thomas Potter, who was engaged on a biological study of the races. "From a study of specimens I believe that the Celts = Untrustworthy and Blacks = Savages. *Ergo* Both Destined to Die in Great Conflagration. We should mount a joint expedition. I have heard there is a boat for charter."

"Cape Town is a lousy place," snarled Kewley. "What use is a free port to a smuggler? We'll be better off in Hobart."

"Look at those scuttering white pissers," thought Peevay, the half-caste Aborigine. "I should have speared them like Mother said."

"Will you be our guide?" asked Rev Wilson.

"No, I won't do that."

"I hear he's changed his mind," said Dr Potter, several days later.

"It was that red-beard shitter Potter that made off with Mother's body," Peevay said to himself, "and none of the other nums would lift a finger to help a black fellow. I will kill them."

"So near, yet so far to Eden," Rev Wilson repeated deliriously.

"Wilson = quite deranged" wrote Potter in his diary. "No food left = big problem. We have lost Ben Fiddler. Hooper suggesting could = work of half-caste."

"Scuttering shitters," said Peevay, "I'd have had the nums if the ship hadn't come."

"You go somewhere remote to do a bit of running business and you bump into these fritlags again," mused Captain Kewley, as Wilson and Potter came aboard.

"The Lord has saved us," intoned Wilson.

"It looks as if we got away with it," said Kewley on his return to London, as he spotted a skeleton labelled Aboriginal at an exhibition that showed every sign of having had a red beard.

The digested read ... digested

The doctor, the vicar, the smuggler and the Aborigine venture into Tasmania's Heart of Darkness

Transmission

Hari Kunzru

Arjun had dreamt of Silicon Valley when he was living in India, but a San Francisco bedsit had never featured. The job that had been promised him had never materialised. No one wanted to employ him when they discovered he was on a temporary visa.

His mother rang. "I've just been promoted," he lied, before rewinding his tape of Leela Zahir *in Naughty Naughty, Lovely Lovely* and watching it for the 27th time.

* * *

Guy Swift was feeling pleased with himself, but then caricatures like him always do at the start. He had the marketing media agency, Tomorrow, the flash apartment, the beautiful girl.

* * *

Things were looking up for Arjun. He had been hired by Virugenix and was working in the holy of holies. Pay wasn't great but it was a start.

* * *

The pitch in New York had failed. The venture capitalists were asking questions; the money was running out fast.

"I'm leaving you," said Gaby.

Guy swallowed hard. First the business, now the girl.

* * *

"We're making you redundant," said Daryll.

"But you can't," pleaded Arjun. He returned to his studio and picked out a disk. It was time to show them how much he was needed.

* * *

The first Leela virus found its way around the ether in less than 12 hours. In the course of a week, nine global businesses were badly disrupted. The experts concluded that it was the work of terrorists.

* * *

For no good reason Rocky Prasad decided to make a Bollywood film in Scotland with Leela Zahir as the leading lady. For no good reason Leela refused to leave her room. So for no good reason, Gaby, the publicist, had sex with the leading man.

* * *

Arjun was sweating. The net was closing in. He made a video for Leela, before making a break for Canada.

* * *

The Pan European Border Agency (PEBA) had fallen for Guy's obvious bullshit and would sign tomorrow. After celebrating, he disappeared.

* * *

Leela watched the young man explain how he had meant no malice in using her image for his virus. He was quite cute. She disappeared.

* * *

Arjun had headed south by mistake. But Mexico would do. The FBI surrounded his room. Shots were fired, but the dead body was later identified as a Chinese teenager. Arjun had disappeared.

* * *

Guy washed up on an Italian beach. He had been wrongly identified as an illegal immigrant after the Leela virus infected the PEBA system and was deported to Albania. He was never the same again. Leela and Arjun were never seen again. The conspiracy theorists had a field day.

The digested read ... digested

A promising story gets sidetracked by a virus and everything goes rapidly downhill

Thinks

David Lodge

One, two, testing I'm recording the thoughts going through my head Got a good snog from Marianne Better keep the tape hidden from Carrie.

So here I am. Teaching creative writing at Gloucester University. God I feel lonely since Martin died. People are being kind, though, and Ralph and Carrie Messenger seem to have adopted me.

I really fancy Helen Reed. I must read her book and try to manipulate a way of meeting her on campus.

"Hi, I was just passing," said Carrie. "Would you like lunch?"

"So what is cognitive science?" asked Helen over a salad.

"It's the study of consciousness. Is it just electrochemical activity in the brain? Can feelings be reduced to hard-wiring? In short, how to give an objective account of a subjective phenomenon."

"Novelists have been doing that for years," replied Helen.

Ralph thought he had manipulated our meeting. Actually, I had been hanging around hoping he would make a move. I thought he might kiss me when he left.

I contemplated giving Helen a kiss, but thought it a bit obvious.

I'm completely thrown. The sex scenes in one of my students' works could only have been written by someone who had been to bed with Martin.

"I wasn't the first," she said when I confronted her.

"Will you go to bed with me?" asked Ralph. "No. I don't approve of adultery."

She had left a pair of knickers out accidentally on purpose.

I turned Ralph down, but it was a closer call than he realises.

If only I could be sure Carrie wouldn't find out.

Helen keeps a diary. That's interesting.

My God. I bumped into Carrie in Ledbury. She's having an affair with Nick, the interior designer.

"Carrie's gone off to the States as her dad's ill. Can I come round?"

"OK."

I haven't had such good sex in years. I think I'm getting fond of him.

The sex is great. I hope Carrie doesn't find out.

"I've got a lump. The doctor says it might be cancerous. I can't see you for a while."

"I understand," Helen replied.

He's withdrawing from me.

This is getting messy. I'm going to have to back off from her.

"I haven't got cancer after all. I'll see you around."

"I understand."

The digested read ... digested

Cogito, ergo shag

Atonement

Ian McEwan

Briony gazed out the window at the leonine yellow sunlight reflecting off the fiery gravel. How could she have let herself be outmanoeuvred by her cousin Lola? As her fury abated – self-pity was so unattractive, especially in a 13-year-old – Briony spied her sister Cecilia talking to Robbie. As Briony imagined their conversations, Cecilia undressed to her undergarments before diving into the water. What turmoil of emotions had possessed her?

Robbie and Cecilia had been friends since childhood, but had grown apart at Cambridge. How best to convey his feelings without invoking contrition or hauteur? True, he no longer felt deference to her class, but could it be he was ashamed by his attraction? "I want to kiss your cunt," he wrote. There, for his eyes only, he had admitted the truth.

"Run along and give this to Cee," said Robbie to Briony. Only as he entered the house, did he realise he had slipped the wrong letter into the envelope.

"I am most dreadfully sor" he began as Cecilia approached. His words were cut off by her rampant tongue. Briony interrupted their passion. How violent he looked, Briony thought.

"I've been attacked," sobbed Lola later that evening.

"It was Robbie," exclaimed Briony.

* * *

Robbie saw a child's limb dangle from a tree as he headed towards Dunkirk. The shrapnel wound in his side jagged on his belt, leaking blood and pus. Three and a half years in prison for a rape he didn't commit compounded his bitterness. He had to make it home, back to Cecilia.

Briony changed the putrid dressing. She had abandoned writing to become a nurse. Her first efforts had been rejected by Elizabeth Bowen for being too derivative of Virginia Woolf – now she must atone for her sins. Cecilia had never answered her letter, so she visited unannounced. "I'm sorry," she said, as Robbie stepped out from behind the door.

* * *

Sixty years have passed and soon all the protagonists will be dead, thought Briony as she left for a celebration of her life in letters. Only then, can the truth be told. This is my final draft. What would be served by persuading you that Robbie died at Dunkirk and Cecilia in the Balham Underground disaster? I want them to be happy. But what really happened? How can the novelist achieve atonement when she is also God?

The digested read ... digested

The Oxford Companion to 20th-century English literature

Black Swan Green

David Mitchell

Moron, grinny-zitty as ever. His bumfluff's getting thicker, mind.

His real name's Dean Moran and I'd call him Dean if we were on our own but it would be gay to call him that now because names aren't just names. My name is Jason Taylor, though I write poetry for the parish magazine under the name Eliot Bolivar 'cos poetry is gay. It's tough being 13 and having no real voice of my own. Sometimes I feel like I'm a 35-year-old man who's trying too hard to be knowing. I was going to say self-conscious, but Hangman would get me.

I call it Hangman because that's what I was playing when my stammer first started. I go and see a speech therapist now and sometimes it's better and sometimes it's not and most times I just try and use another word. It's Ss and Ds that catch me out.

It's 1982 and I feel the need to namecheck as many things as possible so you'll know I'm real. Epic. *The Human League, 2000AD, Chariots of Fire, Space Invaders*. I'm stuck up a tree watching as Tom Yew's body jerkjerked judderily jackknifed on Debby Crombie. He's home on leave from *HMS Coventry*. So you can take it as read he's going to die in the Falklands in 100 pages' time.

Maggot. You plonker, screamed the UnbornTwin, as the mad old woman from the woods appeared. And here's the Badger. I seem to be spawning more voices. Help me, David, things are getting out of hand. Dad's snorey-skonks and flobberglobbers're impossible to sleep through. Thanks.

They say nothing changes at Black Swan Green. Even the joke that there are no swans gets repeated. But things are changing at home. Dad's being ever so polite to Mum these days and he's given me a TV for my bedroom. Something's wrong? Yet I still can't tell him I've broken Grandad's watch.

I get an invite to the vicarage. "I want to help you with your poetry," said Madame Crommelynck. "If you are not truthful to the world, your world will stink of falseness." Jesus, where did that come from? "Mme Crommelynck has been deported back to Germany," says the vicar. Epic.

Except my cousin Hugo says no one says epic any more. I wouldn't mind, but things are racing – I was going to say speeding – out of control. I can't keep Dawn Madden out of my mind and she's going out with Ross Wilcox who's given me a kicking for being gay enough to go to the cinema with my mum who's got a job working in Cheltenham and I've found Ross's wallet at the fairground and I don't want to give it back to him 'cos Dawn has just dumped him and he's lost £600 of his dad's money and I could buy another watch but then I give it back and Ross goes mad 'cos he sees Dawn snogging Grant Burch and he crashes a motorbike and loses a leg and it's, like, all my fault.

Deep breath. Ground me, Maggot.

"Your mother and I are splitting up," says Dad. "And don't worry about the watch."

I grind Neil Broase's calculator in the vice. Suddenly I don't care about the bullies any more and I'm moving home and Holly Deblin gives me my first ever snog. Tongues. I can sense it's the end but there is no end.

The digested read ... digested

The – I was going to say secret – diary of Jace Taylor, aged 13 and a half

The Autograph Man

Zadie Smith

Alex-Li feels a little left out as Rubinfine and Adam lock fingers. He starts chatting to the boy sitting next to him at the Big Daddy wrestling match. "Hi, *I'm* Alex-Li Tandem," he says.

"Joseph Klein," the boy replies, "I collect autographs."

"Oh look," gasps Alex-Li, as he watches Li-Jin collapse. "My father's just died. Maybe I'll *collect* autographs, too."

* * *

Alex-Li had been in bed for three days. That was some Superstar microdot. He stretched his legs and took in the north-west London air. In the distance he caught sight of Rabbi Rubinfine.

"How *are* you doing?" he asked.

"Why do you always talk in italics?" the Rabbi replied.

"Dunno. *I've* got this odd stylistic *tic*."

"Let's talk about being Jewish."

"Why?"

"Is that not all that Jewish people talk about?"

Alex-Li dropped in on Adam.

"Esther's unhappy with you," said Ads.

"Can't help that. I've finally *been* sent a genuine Kitty Alexander."

"You've been taking too many drugs, man, no one's got a Kitty."

Alex-Li went to Cotterell's to verify some autographs. It was the first time he had seen Boot since ending their affair.

"Boot, *meet* Joseph and Rubinfine," said Alex-Li, as they got to his flat.

"We've met."

"You bastard, Joseph," yelled Alex-Li, "you've had an affair *with*

Boot, too, and told Esther *about* mine."

Jesus, thought Alex-Li as he checked his messages. I must have booked a flight to New York while I was out of it. Still, it will go down well with US readers. He phoned Ads. "I'm *off* to New York."

"You'll miss Esther's heart operation."

"*Hmm*. That adds some pathos."

"Hi, Kitty."

"How did you track me down when thousands of other autograph hunters haven't managed it in 40 years?"

"It wasn't too hard. Now that I've got you away *from* your manager, Max, come with me to London and cash in."

"Esther, meet Kitty. I've just made her £150K."

"We'll get on fine. But I still don't know whether I want to get back with you."

"I think I still miss *my* dad."

"Recite the Kaddish," said Rubinfine.

The digested read ... digested

Alex-Li Tandem survives a bad-name day, a bad trip and a raft of unlikely coincidences to discover celebrity has its price

The Finishing School

Muriel Spark

Of the eight fee-paying students at College Sunrise in Lausanne, Chris was the only one to give Rowland disquiet. Nina and Rowland had always been agreed that the whole purpose of the enterprise was Rowland's novel. Yet while his lay largely unwritten, his red-headed student's advanced swiftly.

"He's only 17," Nina comforted. "It's probably rubbish."

Rowland was not convinced. He had asked Chris if he could read his manuscript, and had been turned down. Worse still, Rowland had alerted Chris to his interest and the student had now passed on his work to Pallas for safe-keeping.

"Do you find your characters have a life of their own?" Rowland enquired one day.

"No, they do only what I tell them."

Rowland damned Chris for his self-assurance. How dare he directly contradict the third lecture of Rowland's creative writing course?

"It's hard to find a publisher for your kind of work," Rowland added spitefully.

"I already have a couple who are interested and I'm talking to someone about the film rights this weekend."

As the months passed, Nina began to resent her husband's paralysis.

"You've got to do something about your jealousy. Maybe you should spend some time in a monastery."

"Well, you've been having an affair with Dr Brown." Which was true, but then Nina had been planning her exit from the marriage and would one day go on to wed Dr Brown and become an art historian.

After three weeks alone in the seminary, Rowland felt the grip of his obsession loosen. There was a knock on his door.

"Come back. I need you," Chris implored. "I can't write without your jealousy."

The torture returned. "I'm going to have to kill him," Rowland confided to Nina.

The well-known publisher Monty Fergusson arrived in town. "Would you like to come along to meet him? Chris asked Rowland.

"I've read your novel," said Fergusson. "Obviously it's shit, but as you're 17 it will be quite saleable if I can get a good editor to work on it."

Fergusson died a few weeks later, but his opinion had got around and interest in Chris's work began to dissipate. Only one publisher, Grace Formby, held firm. She, too, thought Chris's age was marketable, but was more taken with the idea of Rowland's observations of teaching in a Swiss finishing school.

"You bastard," yelled Chris, as he barged in on Rowland relaxing in his bath. "You've turned the publishers against me." He picked up the electric fire. Rowland jumped out of the bath and tried to grab him.

Chris's book received reasonable notices on its publication, as did Rowland's. Chris joined Rowland at the college and after a year they engaged in a same-sex affirmation ceremony.

The digested read ... digested

The old ones are often the best

The Light of Day

Graham Swift

Evenin' all.

We all step near the line at one time or another, but few cross it. Tonight's episode is about what happens when the line is crossed.

* * *

Reet looks at me strangely. She knows where I'm going. Today is a special day. It's two years ago exactly since it happened.

* * *

"My husband's having an affair," said Mrs Nash.

Private investigators hear this sort of thing all the time. I let her carry on talking.

"He's been sleeping with Kristina, a Croatian refugee, we took in," she – Sarah, let's call her Sarah – continued. "She's going home now. He's taking her to the airport. I want you to see that he doesn't go with her."

"Are you sure you want to know?" I ask. People often don't really want to know the truth.

* * *

What if she had said no? Where would we all be now? I laid the flowers on Robert Nash's grave. Have you any words for me, Rob? Silence. I'm good at silence. I said nothing to my mum when I discovered my father was having an affair.

* * *

I reached Kristina's flat in Fulham shortly after 4pm. The two of them left the flat at about 5pm, got into his black Saab and proceeded in a westerly direction down the M4. They turned off at the Heathrow spur and parked at Terminal 2. Kristina walked through the departure gate, without looking back.

* * *

They treat me differently at the prison. They know I'm an ex-police officer. They think I'm corrupt, but all I was trying to do was nail that bastard Dyson. I knew he was guilty. So did everyone else, but we didn't have the evidence so it was my head on the block. My wife, Rachel, left me soon after. Any excuse.

* * *

The doors open and I walk into the visiting-room. She's sitting down already.

"Hello, sweetheart," I say. "I'll be waiting for you when you get out."

* * *

I don't know why I decided to follow him home. Would anything different have happened if I hadn't? Maybe she wouldn't have seen what I had seen. And I wouldn't have been able to write this book. Nor you to read it. So much rests on our choices.

I had seen the emptiness in his eyes. He had gone back to their house in Wimbledon but his heart was on the plane. Sarah had been cooking him supper when she saw those eyes. So she stabbed him to death.

* * *

I return to my office. Reet had told me it would fade. But it hasn't. One day I won't be a visitor any more. And I won't return alone.

So remember folks: Wimbledon is still very safe; unless you cross the line. Mind how you go, now.

The digested read ... digested

The quantum theory of suburbia

Lighthousekeeping

Jeanette Winterson

I have no father. There's nothing unusual about that. Not long after I was born, I didn't have a mother, either. We lived in a house on a hill in Salts on the northern coast of Scotland. She fell down the hill and died.

"You're going to live with Pew in the Cape Wrath lighthouse," said Miss Pinch.

"You must be blind," I said to my new guardian.

"How did you guess?"

"I've read this sort of pretentious crap before."

"Let me tell you a story," he said, "a story that has no end."

"I was rather hoping it had no beginning, too."

Pick a date. Any date. 1811. That's the year Robert Stevenson completed the Bell Rock lighthouse. Take another year. 1802. See, the story doesn't really have a beginning. Josiah Dark came to Salts to supervise the building of the lighthouse. Robert Stevenson had a relative who wrote *Treasure Island*. The Pews have always been lighthouse keepers: Pew feels as if he has been there forever. "I'm over 160 years old," he said nonchalantly. My dog nodded in understanding. See, everything can be interconnected if you're happy to write bollocks.

Tell me another story. Josiah had a son, Babel. By all accounts Babel was a happy man living in Bristol. Everyone thought he would marry his girlfriend Molly. But Molly got pregnant. Babel thought she had slept with another man and fled to Salts to become a pastor. He was not a happy man: he married a woman he did not love and hit her from time to time. He fled Salts for two months every year.

No one knew where he went. In fact, he spent the time with Molly. He was so happy with her, he called himself Mr Lux in Bristol. Back in Salts he called himself Mr Dark. See, it's just like *Dr Jekyll and Mr Hyde* ... Please stop. You promised there were no endings.

Pew got a letter saying the lighthouse was to be automated. I woke to find my dog rowing him out to sea. Pew was singing, "I'm gonna live for ever. I'm gonna learn how to fly." Tell me another story.

I went to Capri. I tried to steal a bird that talked to me. But I got caught. The end. Except there are no ends.

Tell me a story. The story of life. Dark found a cave full of fossils. Charles Darwin came to examine them. Could the world really have begun with the flood, thought Dark. The beginning. Deep.

Tell me a story about a story. I tried to read *Death in Venice* in the library. But the librarian took it home. I didn't want to buy a copy so I never got to finish it. The middle. Deeper.

And then I met you in Greece. We fell in love. I love you, I love you. We came back to the lighthouse. There was Pew and my dog. "We told you there were no endings," they chorused.

But thankfully there are.

The digested read ... digested

No beginnings, no middle and no endings, but you've still read it all before

The Book of Dave

Will Self

JUN 523 AD (dating from the discovery of *The Book of Dave*): Carl
Dévúsh debouched into the moto wallows.

– Should ve go 2 ve Ferbiddun Zön?

– We have to, said Antonë Bom in perfect Arpee. Because there
we will find the second Book of Dave.

– Pleath don urt me, whispered the moto as ve Daddies and ve
opares started ve flensing. Ve mummies stud 2 1 syde as it wuz
na ye Chanjovadá. The Lawyer and the Driver paraded Carl and
Antone before the Hamstermen.

– All Fliars R sent frum ve Geezer an mus suffah on ve Weel.

DECEMBER 2001: Dave Rudman powered his cab left up Park
Lane, round Marble Arch and up towards Hampstead.

– *I fuckin ate foreigners, posh twats an most of all I ate Chell*, he
thought. *Ow dar she na le mi C Carl.*

SEP 509 AD: – Eye'v sussed ve nu way, said Symun. *Ve Book of Dave*
wot prevents mummies an daddies livin togevver iz wrong. E l8ta
rote anuvver book wich sed mummies an daddies mus B togevver.

– Shu ya chavvish mouff, replied ve Driver. *Ve Book of Dave* is
ve Nolidj.

JUNE 1987: Michelle couldn't forgive Cal for treating her so badly
as she rode home. She looked at the driver. He was a bit fat, bit bald
but nice enough. The next January she turned up on Dave's doorstep,
seven months pregnant.

KIPPER 522 AD: - Ware R we goin? asked Carl.

– Nu Lundun, replied Antone.

– Y?

– Coz sumfinks go 2 appun.

AUGUST 2002: Dave sat down next to Fukka Funch at the Fighting Fathers meeting.

– Is no rí vat ve courts av stopped mí goin neer Chell an Cal's gaff. U no wo? Lass ni I wen an berried a buk Ive rittun in vere gardun so a least Carl mite 1 da no wot I feel. Chanjovadays? My arse.

MAR 523 AD: It was the third tarrif and the headlight was fullbeam as Carl and Antonë made their way along the Emwun into New London.

– I still doan no wot were doin, Carl moaned.

– U mus na ask questions, whispered Antone. Vis iz ment 2 B a cleva satyre on receevd relidjun in a post-apoclpytic Ingerlund.

– I wurkd vat 1 aht donkeys ago. But weres ve storí?

– Vere isunt 1. U R just men 2 B dazzled by ve ventwilkwism.

FEBRUARY 2003: Dave was detoxing from the Seroxat and the Zopiclone.

– Ah must av bin aht of mí ed wen I berried vat rant in ve gardun. Now I doan even mind vat much that Carl iz Cal's sun, an na myne.

– You could write to Carl explaining to him what you really feel now, said Antony Bohm, Dave's psychiatrist.

JUN 524 AD:

– Ere we R bak on Ham, said Carl. An veyve killd all ve motos.

– Vey dun it coz Symun the Geezer wuz ur Dad, replied Antonë. It's ve en ov uz fliars. Dävism is now ve onlee Dävinanity.

OCTOBER 2003: Cal, Carl and Chell gathered around Dave's graveside.

– Maybe we should bury his letter near to his rant, Cal said.

– Whateffa, Carl laughed. Ahm gonna B a lawyer not a cabby. Sides snot Dave's Will, It's Will's Dave.

The digested read ... digested

Mockní Rebul

The digested read ...

Memoirs

The Beatles Anthology

The Beatles

John: Penny Lane is a suburban district where I lived with my mother, father and grandfather. When I was 12 I thought I was a genius. Rock'n'roll was real and Paul and I hit it off straight away.

Paul: When I wrote "When I'm Sixty-Four", I thought I was writing a song for Frank Sinatra. My dad gave me ten shillings once; that's the only person in my whole life who's ever given me anything for free.

George: My earliest recollection is of sitting at the top of the stairs having a poop – shouting, "finished". As I said in my own book, *I Me Mine*, my earliest memories are of things like "One Meatball" by Josh White. Paul and I met on the bus.

Ringo: My real name is Parkin, not Starkey. Not many people know that.

Paul: John and Stuart thought of the name. We thought the Beatles sounded a bit creepy, but it had a double meaning. Like one of our favourite groups, the Crickets. You know, cricket the game and cricket the grasshoppers.

George: It was a bit of a shambles.

Paul: Now we were truly professional.

John: We were terrible.

Ringo: I never forgave Eddie Cochran for getting killed.

Paul: Hamburg was quite an eye-opener. A sex shock.

John: We thought our songs were a bit wet, but we decided to try them.

Paul: Pete Best was a bit limited.

John: I heard he was glad to have missed becoming one of the four most famous people on the planet.

Ringo: When "Love Me Do" came out we'd stop the car to hear it on the radio.

Paul: In 1964 we only got Nov 23 off.

John: Drugs were around a long time.

George: I was given the *Illustrated Book of Yoga* on my birthday.

Ringo: I'm not sure if we had a joint in the palace or not.

John: It sort of dawned on me that love was the answer.

Paul: *Magical Mystery Tour* wasn't the worst Christmas programme.

John: After Yoko and I met, I didn't realise I was in love with her. Until she told me.

George: It was an establishment plot to get us busted.

Paul: Yoko in the studio created tensions.

John: I started the band. I disbanded it. Simple as that. Good night and thanks for the bread.

The digested read ... digested

The Fab Four look deep inside their bank statements and find the anorak within

Learning to Fly

Victoria Beckham

I was an eight-year-old girl with a dream. I was going to be like one of the kids from *Fame*, and as I thought about the bit where the audience get to dance on stage I had literally never been so excited. And you know what? When my mum took me to see Cliff Richard at Wembley a few months later, I said to her, "I'm going to be performing up there one day." How weird is that?

My mum and dad are literally the best parents in the world, and my sister, Louise, and brother, Christian, are just so my two best friends. I know my fame has been difficult for them but they are just so thrilled at my success. I was never the brightest nor the prettiest girl in school, but I was just so determined. I was going to be famous and nothing was going to stop me, not even lack of talent. How Girl Power is that?

I spotted the ad for an all-female band in *The Stage*, and no one could have been more surprised than me when I was chosen, but when I met the other girls we just gelled. We were just so ALL GIRL.

Everyone was, like, "Where did they come from?" when the Spice Girls released "Wannabe", but we had been literally working round the clock for over a year to make sure our launch was perfect. Then everything went literally berserk. Number 1 after Number 1, hotel room after hotel room; I started losing weight, but it was basically Geri's fault I became anorexic. Not that I was anorexic, because anorexia is just so not me.

I literally didn't know who David was when I first met him. How dim is that? But I soon realised he was the man for me. He is just so sensitive and so not like other footballers.

Geri. Leaving. The. Band. Was. Literally. The. Biggest. Surprise. In. The. World. But I wasn't really surprised as she was a much worse singer and dancer than the rest of us and was struggling to keep up. Our audiences didn't even notice she was missing. How sad is that?

Brooklyn is literally the best baby in the entire universe and David and I just so love him to bits. We are just so at our happiest when it's just the three of us together out shopping at Versace. It hurts me when people say I can't sing. Like, how many millions do I have to earn to prove I can? People often hate those with more talent, but I want you all to know I will carry on making music for as long as you want me.

Victoria XXX

The digested read ... digested

Literally my very own book. How cool is that?

Elizabeth: 80 Glorious Years

Jennie Bond

What's the Queen really like? It's a question I was asked more times than I care to remember during my years of reporting on royalty for the BBC. The answer is that she is a very private person who keeps herself to herself, so I don't really know. But I'm not going to let that stop me writing this book.

Many of us feel that the Queen is remote, but her friends believe she is misunderstood. From my own experience I can say that she finds it hard to know when to be intimate. She once said to me, "Hello, Jennie," and I had to remind her of her place by replying, "It's Ms Bond, ma'am."

Checking through the cuttings files, it seems that Elizabeth was born on April 21, 1926. Showing the fortitude that was to personify her reign, she survived the General Strike a fortnight later, and for much of her childhood Elizabeth played blissfully at home with her sister Margaret and the servants, while her parents fulfilled their royal duties.

The abdication of King Edward VIII altered her life for ever, and with great insight she immediately understood that she was now the heir to the throne. During the war, she was keen to play her part, and in 1945 she learnt how to drive an army truck.

Elizabeth knew that Philip Mountbatten was the man for her from the moment she set eyes on him, but their years of carefree married life together, with their two young children, Charles and Anne, were tragically cut short by the premature death of King George VI. At the age of 25, she became queen.

After leafing through some nice pictures, it's time to take up the story again. This was the new dawn of the Elizabethan age, but life was not easy as the new queen was torn between tradition and modernity. Her sister Margaret had an unhappy relationship with Peter Townsend, and the rumours that her own marriage was in trouble were only quashed with the arrival of Prince Andrew and Prince Edward.

The swinging '60s were a time of change for the Queen, and she soon realised that making the monarchy more accessible did not place it above reproach when she allowed the BBC to make the film, *The Royal Family.* However, the Silver Jubilee celebrations of 1977 marked a return to popularity as huge crowds greeted her wherever she travelled.

Prince Charles's marriage to Diana Spencer should have marked the high-water mark of her reign. Instead it presaged the most turbulent period. Three of her children's marriages ended in divorce, several Commonwealth countries considered becoming republics, and if the Queen believed that 1992 was her "annus horribilis", then 1997 must have been even worse as it nearly ended in mutiny after the royal family misjudged the public's mood after Princess Diana's death.

That the royal family has moved into quieter waters in recent years is in no short measure due to the Queen's willingness to do her duty by opening new buildings throughout the world. She has borne her sadnesses quietly and with great dignity and as she approaches 80, the institution of the monarchy is still a vibrant force in British life. How it will adapt in future is – like the Queen herself – an enigma.

The digested read ... digested

Bond goes On Her Majesty's Secret Service

Straight

Boy George with Paul Gorman

Taking a cab home the other day, the driver said, "Didn't you used to be Boy George?"

"You bitch," I muttered. "I may be a little chubbier than I was, but I'm still famous."

People think I'm motivated by money. But I leave that kind of thing to Madonna, or McDonna, as I like to call her. It's narcissism that drives me. I was recently offered $20,000 for a day's work shooting a commercial. "Why would I take that kind of money to look an idiot," I snapped, "when I do it every day for nothing?"

Not a day goes by without someone telling me that my first book, *Take It Like a Man*, was the most significant event of their lives. So I thought I owed them another. I've changed a lot recently. I used to think the world revolved around me; now I know it does.

Having been to India, I am a deeply spiritual person and I can usually tell exactly what someone is thinking about me before they know themselves. I couldn't have reached this state of serenity without so many people, like my good friends Mike and Dragana, reminding me of how important I am to them.

Nine Ki has also been profoundly influential on my life. Every person has three numbers based on their birth date and this dictates how well you can communicate with others. My numbers are 317 which means I am open and kind. Madonna is a 683. Enough said.

I have always been happy with my sexuality, but don't think I've always managed to bed every man I've fancied. My therapist tells me some men find it difficult to cope with how wonderful I am. Sometimes I think the whole world should go into therapy so I could be less misunderstood.

What really upsets me is when men try to forget they have been my lover. Over the years I've had public battles with Jon Moss and Kirk Brandon over this. They both want to move on with their lives. But if you don't want to appear in the gossip columns, don't sleep with a media tart. They are both commitment-phobic or, as my therapist says, in that Egyptian river. Denial.

You might think I've done nothing for the past ten years. In fact, I've played records in clubs, gone on 1980s revival tours, and written and performed in the musical *Taboo*. So many people have told me my portrayal of Leigh Bowery is breathtaking. My therapist believes the reason it closed so quickly in London and New York was that critics couldn't process their envy of my talent.

At times like that, you just have to have a good cry and start again. Already friends are telling me I'm a brilliant photographer and fashion designer. But it's my poetry I always come back to.

Are you happy?
Not all the time,
They'd lock me up for the laughing crime!

The digested read ... digested

Boy George regresses still further, to King Baby

Alan Clark Diaries: Into Politics 1972–1982
Alan Clark

Been v-depressed. The moat's leaking and Hoare's are pressing me to reduce the o/d. Debts now total £80,000 AGAIN. What if the Tate defaults on the Saltonstall? Took a couple of 1000mg Redoxons but am still not a well man. Temperature of 99.3 and feel shattered, *epuisé*. It's probably my prostate. Caught sight of myself in the mirror. So lined, so grey, so old. Despite this I still feel healthily randy. If only the blondes hadn't dumped me.

* * *

Back to Plymouth for constituency business. God, I loathe the place. They haven't liked me much since I openly lent my support to Enoch. Will no one stand up for Britishness? If APC quits Folkestone, I'll try my luck there.

* * *

My political career is not progressing. I don't mind being snubbed by John Patten, who is so ambitious he wouldn't dream of acknowledging any inferior, but Ian Gow walked straight past me. Should I be reading anything into this?

* * *

Met Uncle Harold on my way out of the Commons. "Off to my club," the old PM said. "Whites or Brooks?" I asked. "The Carlton, you fool," he snapped. Is this a good sign? Went to Brooks where I lost £742 at backgammon.

I'm not at all well. My back is playing up and the tip of my penis is quite numb. Had a small spot of bother with a woman who was threatening to go to the papers. Asked Jonathan Aitken what

I should do. "Pay her off," he advised. I gave her £5,000. JA said he would have bargained for £4,000.

Let it be known in a roundabout way that Francis Pym could be next PM. He visibly swelled. Ian invited me for a drink with Margaret. An extraordinarily attractive woman. A few signs of getting a little broad in the beam, though. Hope she doesn't adopt the dowager look.

Made a speech that was rather well received. Worried about using the word, "insouciance", but the papers picked up on it and like it. Jotted down a few *pensées d'escalier* for the *Telegraph*.

Ian implied I might be in line for Margaret's PPS. How loathsome Lawson, oily Gummer and totally bonkers Joseph will have to crawl. For me it will be a K, the FO and the leadership.

Career is not progressing. Passed over in reshuffle. Lost £491 at backgammon. Must stop. I'm not at all a well man.

The digested read ... digested

More sex, lies and hypochondria from the most entertaining political diarist since Chips Channon

Jade: My Autobiography

Jade Goody

A Mariah Carey concert. Better even than East 17. Mariah throws me a big ball thing. Everyone thought I was going to be Mariah Carey when I went on *Celebrity Stars in Their Eyes*, but my agent told me to do Lynn Anderson instead (whoever she is), and I even went up to Cat Deeley and said, "Tonight Matthew, I'm . . ." How braindead is that? But I won anyway. So I can do something, and sod the lot of you.

Who would have thought I'd ever be famous? When I heard them shouting "Pig" outside the *Big Brother* house, I just wanted to sob. But then Davina told me I was a star, and I nudged her and replied, "More than can be said for you."

My dad was a heroin addict and never gave me anything except a couple of things that he nicked. He told my mum his name was Cyrus, so she went and had his name tattooed on her arm and then she found out he was called Antony, after all. Still, she recently had a Hollywood and a butterfly tattooed on her la-la, so it doesn't seem so bad now.

I used to roll joints for my mum when I was four years old because I've always wanted to be helpful, and my mum gave me a huge kiss after I managed to hide all the stolen chequebooks in the freezer when the police raided us. I've always loved my mum, even when people took the piss out of her for being a one-armed lesbian.

Of course, my mum wasn't always a lesbian and she tells me she never goes down on women herself, she just likes having it done to her. She says her arm got paralysed when she had an accident on the back of my Uncle Budgie's motorbike. When we got compensation from the council, we got loads more friends and even went to Egypt, which was minging because there was too much sand.

I'm getting a bit ahead of myself here. I wasn't much good at school and my first sex was with a bloke I gave a hand job to, which was well disgusting. I got better at it though and after I got done for shoplifting – not my fault as I walked out of a shop without paying by mistake and when I saw how easy it was I naturally decided to go back and take a whole lot more stuff on purpose – I had four boyfriends on the go at once. Two of 'em were called Danny and the other two were both called Matthew.

So when I went on *Big Brother* my life was in a bit of a state, especially as my Mum had taken up with a crack addict. I don't remember much about the life in the house as I was well pissed and how embarrassing was it to discover I had given PJ a blow job? And I do know where East Angular is now. It's parked outside Tesco.

Everyone was well and truly gutted – especially that two-faced minger Kate – when I became the most famous contestant, even though I didn't win. I loved it, though.

Today, my life has never been better. It's a shame my relationships with Jeff and Ryan never worked out, and I'm still struggling with bulimia after the toothbrush slipped down my throat. But I've got two beautiful boys, I've been on TV a lot, and I've got my own beauty salon called Ugly's. What more could a girl want?

The digested read ... digested

The stream of unconsciousness

The Year of the Jouncer

Simon Gray

Here I am sitting at my table in the hotel in Barbados. Another Christmas over, thank God. Whenever I think of people I love, I can't stop myself wondering which bit of me is going to pack up first. Tumours here, liver failure there, but otherwise everything is much the same as

The self itself

when I was born. I found I could bounce around in my pram. Jouncing they called it. So a jouncer I was. I don't know why I put that in really. I suppose that writing's become a bit of a habit and people seemed to like the chaos of *The Smoking Diaries* so I thought I might as well carry on. Daddy was a bit of a philanderer and I once hit a cricket ball so hard it would have killed a baby if it had hit it on the head.

My battle with the waves

Sometimes I go swimming and sometimes I don't. Harold and Antonia are joining us today. I'm going to try and wait ten minutes before showing him my new play, *The Old Masters*. I see a strange man standing at the urinal and he reminds me very much of someone I can't quite remember.

What was he talking about?

The play I gave Harold wasn't actually a new one but an old one I'd rewritten. He says he loved it, but I'm not sure if I heard him right, because he said he would direct it if no one else wanted to. I smoke two cigarettes and am inspired to ramble on for several pages about growing up in Nova Scotia, though I can't exactly recall if I've ever been there.

How did we get there?

Yesterday I couldn't recall how we got to the premiere of Simon Callow's revival of my play, *The Holy Terror*. But now I remember we went by car. How strange. The reviews were awful and the play will close soon. I feel dreadfully guilty because I don't even know if the play's any good as I normally just start writing about any old thing that comes to mind and keep on going till I've run out of paper.

All my shirts

have cigarette burns, but I only get my hair cut twice a year. I am getting very worried about my memory and have set myself a task of seeing if I can get to the end of a paragraph without a Diet Coke, I mean losing my train of did I mention that I spent some time with Alan Bates before he died?

Harold Pinter

is directing *The Old Masters* and it appears to be a success. Victoria says this is not good for my image so I smoke seven cigarettes and go the launch of *The Smoking Diaries*. My publisher looks pleased and says can he have more of the same and I say I don't know what you mean and he says that's the idea

Would mummy have wanted me to be gay?

I don't think she would and I've never felt gay though I did once have a crush on a boy. I think I'm losing the plot though I'm not sure you can lose something you never had. The doctor says I have a terminal illness but I've even failed to die. Is there anything I can get right? Till the same time next year . . .

The digested read ... digested

The Year of the Chancer

Jordan: A Whole New World
Katie Price

"I don't love you any more, Katie." Peter's words cut me like a knife and tears streamed down my face.

"You can't mean it," I said. "I love you."

"It's all right, baby," cooed Peter. "You were only dreaming."

I curled back contentedly on to his strong hairless chest – I do like a man who looks after himself!! Back, sac and crack – know what I mean, girls? Who would have thought that I would meet the man of everyone's dreams on a TV reality show?

Even though I was in a long-term relationship with Scott, I knew Pete was the man for me the moment I set eyes on him, and it was torture waiting to see if he had the same feelings for me as I had for him. I sent Scott a text saying "It's over, small willy", and asked Pete's PA to give him my Phil Collins CD. Surely then he could see how much I loved him?

Pete called me the next day. "I love that Phil Collins CD," he said.

I rushed round to his hotel. Somehow I just knew I was going to break my golden rule of not shagging on the first date! Again!!

Pete was in the shower and I knelt before him.

"You just blow me away, babe," he purred.

It would spoil any media deals if we were photographed together, so we had to fly back from Australia separately. Those 24 hours away from Pete were the hardest of my life, but it was lovely to get home to see Harvey again after nearly a month away. I cuddled him for at least ten minutes! Then Pete rang and I rushed to be by his side. We stayed in bed for two days, pleasuring one another. He's just so big, so strong, so dickalicious!

"You complete me, Pete," I said, staring straight into his eyes.

"You complete me too, babe," he replied, staring straight at the TV. "See that bird. I shagged her once, you know."

I flew into a rage and kicked the TV. I'm an extremely jealous woman, and I can't bear the fact that Pete has had sex with so many women. Especially when they are all brunettes with small boobs!

For the first time, I felt truly settled and it wasn't long before I got pregnant. Pete and I were the happiest couple in the world. Apart from a few arguments about his parents and his exes!

I had switched to Pete's manager, Claire, after *I'm a Celebrity…* and she suggested I become a pop star. I cried and cried when Javine was chosen for *Eurovision* instead of me. What a bitch she is, though I have nothing against her personally and wish her all the best.

It was hard bonding with the cameras again after Junior was born, but luckily I had my wedding to plan. It was a real hassle having *OK!* involved but I was very grateful to *OK!* for giving me the chance to be a princess in front of all my celebrity friends.

Pete is the only man who's ever seen me without my hair extensions and I know we are going to stay together for ever and ever. Now, my focus is back on my career. Time to get my boobs done again, guys!!

The digested read … digested

Sheer insaniaty

The Autobiography

Ned Sherrin

I was born between the villages of High and Low Ham in the county of Somerset, and for many years I nursed the dream of becoming Lord Sherrin of Ham. But sadly Donald Sinden beat me to it.

My early memories jostle, a disappointing kaleidoscope of unrequited fumblings with other boys and an absence of interesting people. Things looked up when I went to Oxford to read jurisprudence: here I joined the university dramatic society and met Maggie Smith – still searching for her voice – and Patrick Dromgoole, later head of Harlech TV. Looking through my old programme notes I see I was also acquainted with Nigel Lawson and Ken Tynan.

The theatrical connections I made soon found me living in digs in Chelsea with Peter Nichols and Julian Pettifer and dining at Caletta's, a favoured haunt of Gladys Calthrop, Noel Coward's designer, and Sybil Thorndike.

Walking along the Strand after a performance of *The Matchmaker* at the Haymarket, I bumped into Stephen Wade, who had been a BBC floor manager for the Oxford revue. "Would you like to earn £950 a year working for commercial television?" he asked. And so I found myself producing and directing Tommy Trinder, Noele Gordon, who had been understudying the Ethel Merman role in *Call Me Madam*, Val Parnell and Tyrone Power – among others – for ATV.

A move to the BBC was soon on the cards and while working on the Tonight programme with Jonathan Miller, a very pert Diana Rigg and the Queen of Denmark, I began my long and fruitful writing collaboration with Caryl Brahms, starting with the musical, *Parasol*.

I languished for some time among the cutting rooms of light entertainment alongside Kenneth Milne-Buckley, before I was taken on as a producer for *That Was the Week That Was*. David Frost and I disagree to this day on how I came to choose Ron Grainer to write the signature tune, but it's no exaggeration that TW3 won the 1964 election for Labour.

A brief spell in Hollywood with John Dexter and Zsa Zsa Gabor presaged a return to Somerset to visit my ailing father. Kissing him briefly on the forehead after he had died, I motored back to London to work on three big shows with Caryl Brahms, which gave me the opportunity to direct Sir Donald Wolfit and Dame Flora Robson.

Few people would have predicted the global success of *Side by Side* by Sondheim, but I was happy to cede the narrator's role to Hermione Gingold to work alongside Keith Waterhouse on *Jeffrey Bernard Is Unwell*. Peter O'Toole was a tour de force in the title role and made James Bolam and Dennis Waterman look underpowered in comparison.

Radio critics despise any show that has a glimmer of an idea and *Loose Ends,* the brainchild of Ian Gardhouse, was slated when it was first broadcast but guests such as Elaine Stritch and Frederick Forsyth have ensured its longevity.

Looking through my diaries I see I have failed to mention many of the famous people I have met. Salman Rushdie, Judi, dear Judi Dench, Dorothy Tutin, Nigel Hawthorne . . . I could go on. But my table at Joe Allen awaits.

The digested read ... digested

The arch raconteur

A Mother's Gift

Britney and Lynne Spears

Dusk was beginning to fall as Holly and her mom, Wanda, settled down to watch the *Haverty Talent Hour*.

"Oh Holly, you're so much better than all these singers," sighed Wanda.

"Oh gee," said Holly, looking across at her mom, who would have been the prettiest woman in Biscay were it not for the disfiguring birthmark on her face. "How could an honest but poor Mississippi girl ever go to Haverty, the most expensive performing arts school in the South?"

"Wow," Holly shrieked, "I've got an audition for Haverty."

"I'm not surprised," said Tyler, wiping the grease from his rugged forearms. "You have the finest voice in the world and I took the liberty of sending a tape."

"Oh Tyler," she swooned, kissing his cheek. How they longed to be married so they could go a little further.

"I'm happy to award you the top scholarship," said the college principal, wiping away the tears of deep emotion Holly's singing had induced.

Smoke poured from the dented Chevy as they drove into Haverty's parking lot, which was full of Mercedes. "I'm so ashamed of my mom," thought Holly, "she doesn't even cover up her disfiguring birthmark."

"I've lost her," thought Wanda. "I must remember Ecclesiastes Chapter 3."

"I'm Ditz," said Holly's new roommate, unpacking her Louis Vuitton suitcases. "Don't worry about being poor. You're kinda cute."

They practised choral masterworks and became firm friends.

"Happy birthday, Holly," grinned Ditz as she gave her a pile of designer clothes. "Happy birthday, sweetheart," whispered Wanda as she gave her some pearls. "Puh," thought Holly, "the birthmark has given me some fakes."

"Oh Holly, I'm so miserable," sniffed Ditz. "I may be rich, but my parents don't love me. How I envy the poor but honest closeness of your family."

"I have a confession," said Wanda. "You're adopted. There was a bad fire. I managed to rescue you but your parents were killed. The pearls were theirs."

"Oh gee," cried Holly. "So they weren't fakes and you got the disfiguring birthmark in the fire."

Holly's multi-octave voice soared as she made her debut on the *Haverty Talent Hour*. Everyone wept. "That was for Mom, whose birthmark makes her the most beautiful woman in the world."

The digested read ... digested

The queen of saccharine proves once again that love and a multimillion-pound marketing campaign really can conquer all

The Almond Blossom Appreciation Society

Chris Stewart

Hello boys and girls. It's Friendly Chris here again. You know, the ex-drummer from Genesis you've never heard of who doesn't hold a grudge against Phil Collins and went to live in Spain. Well, I've written another exciting book full of almost-amusing anecdotes about life in Las Alpujarras. So, if you're sitting comfortably, I'll begin.

My friend Michael Jacobs, the art historian, was looking hot and bothered. "I'm double-booked," he gasped. "Is there any chance you could take my group of Bostonians on a tour of the galleries of Seville?"

"But I don't know anything about art," I protested.

"You'll pick it up," he said, nonchalantly.

Luckily, Michael did manage to turn up to do the tour after all, so my lack of knowledge was never exposed. Phew.

Domingo looked down. "*Hola*, Cristobal. Hello, Chris," he muttered in that curious way people in travel books often translate their own sentences. "Antonia's parrot has flown away."

"We'd better find it then," said my wife, Ana, determinedly.

An hour later we'd coaxed the parrot down from the tree. "Mission completed," I smiled. "Let's have a glass of wine and then I'll tend the sheep."

My daughter Chloe had just turned 14 and I was no longer sure how to keep her entertained at El Valero. "Let's go hunting for some frogs," I suggested.

"Whateffa," she yawned. Teenagers, eh? But I know she enjoyed it really!

One day a group of Moroccan refugees appeared at the farm. Spain gets a lot of illegal immigrants and some people aren't very nice to them. I made my Moroccans a nice lunch and they left soon after.

This encounter left me feeling disturbed and I decided to volunteer my services to a charity to help these people. "Maybe I could take the same journey as the North Africans and write about it," I said.

Michael and I set out from Alcala. It was very hot and we got tired. "Why don't we stop for a slice of chorizo?" he said.

"Mmm," I thought. "It's so hard to be authentic. It must be very difficult for the Moroccans." By the way, I went to Morocco once to collect some seeds. What an adventure that was!

We've got a lot of olive trees at El Valero and making the oil can be quite difficult. If you're not careful you can fall out of a tree and hurt yourself. At the end of one season I gave a barbecue for all our friends, and they ate the salads before I had finished cooking the lamb. I was not amused!

"*Por donde andas?*" said Paco. "Where do you walk? Let's go into the hills to smell the almond blossom." What joy!

Mostly it's very hot and dry in the Sierra Nevada, but one winter it snowed. "Let's go skiing," said Gerardo. Completely out of control, I hurtled down the mountain before crashing into a rock. "I've dislocated my shoulder," I moaned ruefully.

Back home, the sheep had got into Ana's vegetable garden. "What shall we do?" I cried. "It's her pride and joy."

"Don't worry," Manolo grinned. "They haven't done much damage."

And now it's time for boys and girls to go to sleep. Oh! You already have.

The digested read ... digested

You had to have been there ...

The Other Side of Nowhere

Danniella Westbrook

> I don't know why
> I don't know what
> Makes me do the things
> I know I should stop

I wrote this poem in 2000. By that stage my addiction to cocaine was so bad I really thought I was going to die and I just wanted my three-year-old son Kai to have some idea of how the most famous drug addict in the world was struggling to cope.

It's easy to blame your parents, but I really did have the happiest childhood a girl could want and Mum and Dad worked hard to give me everything I needed. I was never much interested in school and my mum sent me along to the Sylvia Young Theatre School. Dad wasn't that keen as he wanted me to have an ordinary life, but I was desperate to be on the stage.

Ross and Steve warned me that my world would change when my first episode of *EastEnders* was shown in 1990, but even I didn't imagine how much. Suddenly I had money and I thought I could do anything. I fell in with a bad crowd from south London and started doing cocaine. At first it was fun. Everyone was doing coke at that time, even old people in bingo halls, and it just seemed normal. But before long I was addicted.

People assume that the first time I left the soap I did so under a cloud, but nothing could be further from the truth, as although I was addicted to drugs, my lifestyle didn't get in the way of my work. It was a bit different when I went back to *EastEnders* in 1995, though. By then I had been in rehab once and was going seriously off the rails.

Have I mentioned I was addicted to cocaine? It was even worse when I went back to *EastEnders* for the third and final time in 1999. Mike Read said to me, "Oi princess, that stuff is killing you," and everyone on the cast was great, except for Martine McCutcheon who used to try to cheer me up by singing to me.

I've always said I was never going to write about my boyfriends and I'm not going to start now even though I'm writing my autobiography. All I will say is that someone got me pregnant with Kai and I got married to someone else whom I shortly divorced.

By now I was notorious for being a famous soap star with a drug problem and the paparazzi took a picture of me with part of my nose missing. Cocaine had brought me to my knees. I was lucky now to meet Kevin. Some people thought he was a bit hard, but I always saw the softer side of him and fell in love with him the moment I set eyes on him.

Unfortunately, I was still in the grips of addiction. I was losing weight and struggling to look after Kai and Kevin said he couldn't stay with me till I got better. Things got very bad for a while because cocaine is a dangerous drug, but after one more failed attempt at rehab, I went to the Cottonwood Clinic in Arizona.

I was now ready to get well. My nose has been repaired, Kevin and I have a baby daughter and I have presented one or two forgettable programmes on television. My life has never been better.

The digested read ... digested

A nose for trouble

Chick and lad lit

PS, I Love You

Cecelia Ahern

"It's just so unfair that Gerry got that nasty brain tumour," sobbed Holly. "Together we almost had a personality."

It had been three months since Gerry died and Holly still hadn't got over it. Denise, Sharon and John, her three best friends who also almost had a personality between them, had done their best to be understanding but were starting to get worried. "We're very worried," they all said.

Holly's mother was also very worried and had invited the whole family for lunch to cheer her up. "It's time to pull yourself together," said her older brother Richard, who found himself set up to be the insensitive one. "Why is he so uncaring?" groaned Holly.

"Gerry gave me these letters for you," said Holly's mother. "They are to be opened one by one at the start of each month." Holly rushed home to open the first. "Enter a karaoke competition. PS, I love you." She wept. She'd forgotten how interesting and imaginative Gerry was.

"I hate singing," wailed Holly. Sharon and Denise roared her on as she croaked her way through karaoke night at Hogan's. "You were very brave," whispered Daniel, the bar owner, as he sidled up to Holly. "I've been hurt, too. My girlfriend dumped me and I'm going to feature as your new potential love interest."

Holly opened the next letter. "Get a proper job. PS, I love you," it said. She'd never had a proper job. Maybe now she should shoot for the moon. She looked at the ads. There was her perfect job working on a magazine but she had no experience or qualifications. "I'm going to give you the job because my wife's just died," said the magazine owner. She had shot for the moon – and landed!!

She rushed down to the newsagent. In the queue stood a breathtakingly handsome man, who clearly fancied her. And she fancied him. But it was all too soon. She ran off.

Sharon phoned. "I'm pregnant," she yelled. Holly felt so lonely. Did her friends not realise how difficult things were for her? Denise rang. "I'm getting married," she yelled. Holly felt even more lonely.

"You have to allow other people to move on," Richard whispered. He had become much more caring since he lost his job and his wife left him.

"You're right," she smiled. "We all have to move on."

It was time to open Gerry's last letter. "You must learn to love again. PS, I love you." He was right. But was she ready?

"I really love you, truly and deeply," said Daniel. Was he Mr Right? Would there be a Mr Right? Holly just didn't know. "I need t-time," she s-s-stammered.

It was the last day of the month. Daniel phoned. "I don't love you after all," he said. "I'm back with my ex."

Holly's heart leapt. She ran to the newsagent. There was the breathtakingly handsome man. "I've been waiting 250 pages for you," he cooed. She melted into his eyes. It had been at least ten months since the funeral. Gerry? Gerry who?

The digested read ... digested

Gerry dies before the start and the rest die on the page

The Wonder Spot

Melissa Bank

"Don't you have any other shoes?" says Mum, as we get in the car to go to my cousin's batmitzvah.

"You must have a batmitzvah, too, Sophie," says my mum.

"Don't want one," I reply.

"Well, you could at least go to Hebrew classes," my dad suggests. I go for a while before losing interest.

"OK," says Dad, "you don't have to have a batmitzvah, after all."

At college I share a room with Venice. She'd come from Antibes and was more sophisticated than me. She had a boyfriend and I got to hang out with her a lot. I even met a man who kind of snogged me. Then she left and we never saw each other again.

I move in with my brother Robert and his girlfriend, Naomi, in New York.

"Yuk," says Naomi, "you've mixed up meat and dairy."

"You've got to be more kosher," adds Robert. Since when was he so orthodox? "By the way, we're getting married," they both purr.

"You need to get married," says Grand Mam when I move into her apartment to kind of teach myself to type.

"Whoopee," I cry after six months, "I'm up to nine words a minute." I start going out with Josh. For a long time I didn't care whether he asked me to marry him or not, but then he didn't and I kind of did.

I get a job working for my brother Jack's ex-girlfriend, Honey, at a publishing house. Honey doesn't like me, but that could be because I am always late. I become sort of friends with Francine who reads the slush pile. One day she found a really good book, but I told Honey, who took the credit, and everyone was pissed.

Dad died and Mum kind of changed. I went to spend more time with her in Surrey, Pennsylvania, and almost took a job working on the magazine *Shalom* before I realised I needed to be more religious. I went out with Demetri for a bit, and then we kind of didn't.

I moved back to New York and met Matthew. He reminded me of my father so I decided not to go out with him, but then we kind of did go out for a few pages and then we kind of split up.

Gran died and Mum started dating a married man, which was kind of weird. I took up painting classes and met a man called Bobby. "I know you're trouble," I say, "but I'm going to date you anyway." He doesn't call me for a week and we kind of split. I call Francine. She's OK.

I then met Neil. He was different from the other guys. He loved me for myself. "I want to marry you," he begs.

"You're too needy," I sneer. "Forget it."

I'm now going out with Seth, and I realise I'm kind of jealous of his ex. I don't think we'll get married, so nothing's really changed. And then for no apparent reason I decide I like myself and my job. I have hit the Wonder Spot. The End.

The digested read ... digested

The Girl's Guide to Repetition and Inertia

Wicked!

Jilly Cooper

"You do realise that Larks is a failing school?" Janna tossed back her luxuriant red curls as the governors of Larkminster comprehensive offered her the job of headteacher. "I think it's wicked," she squealed. "And I'm delighted to give Feral, Paris, Kylie, Graffi and other chavs the chance to succeed."

Hengist Brett-Taylor furrowed his handsome brow. Bagley Hall had gone from strength to strength since he had been in charge, but the independent sector could always benefit from associating itself with state schools. And besides, Janna was quite a minx.

"You must be careful, Janna," Hengist purred. "Ashton Douglas and the LEA are looking to close Larks. But I can persuade Randal Stancombe, a local property developer, to buy Larks a minibus so we could put on a joint performance of *Romeo and Juliet*."

Janna moistened. Hengist stood for everything she hated, but how could she resist his bedroom eyes?

"Oh Gawd," drawled Cosmo Supah-Doopah, to his chums Tarquin and Xavier. "The head's only gorn and made us do Shakespeare with the proles. How fraffly orful."

"We think it's great," drooled Milly and Dulcie, the Bagley Babes, their bosoms heaving in anticipation. "The lower orders are well lush."

The production was a triumph, with Paris a sensation as Romeo. "I must offer him a scholarship," Hengist thought, as his fingers gently twanged Janna's suspender-belt.

Janna's head was in a whirl. She wanted Hengist, yet felt guilty about betraying his wife, Sally. If only she could fancy Bagley's moody history teacher, Emlyn; but he only had eyes for Hengist's daughter, Orianna.

Hengist smiled to himself. The *Telegraph* had loved his piece, the opposition wanted him to be education minister and, best of all, the sultry Ruth Walton was going down on him.

Janna wept tears of bitter anguish. How could Hengist betray her and how could Ashton say he was going to close Larks when her working-class pets were making such tremendous strides?

An anonymous cheque for £120,000 arrived on Janna's doorstep. She could afford to keep the GCSE class open after all. A second surprise soon followed.

"I've come to teach history," Emlyn said in his sexy Welsh lilt.

"We've got work to do," yelled Janna, "especially as the sports minister has taken on a bet to see if he can get a GCSE in a year at Larks."

What a year it was. Never had Larks and Bagley Hall seen such heavy petting and frantic coupling. And how Janna's heart swelled with pride when everyone did so well in their exams.

Hengist looked up at Alex Bruce, his deputy. What an odious nonentity he was. "I believe that you cheated on behalf of Paris," Alex snarled. Hengist paled. "It's true, and I've betrayed my wife," he said. "I should go to prison."

"Oh Janna, you've won the National Teaching awards, it was me who sent the £120,000 and I've discovered Orianna is a lesbian," cooed Emlyn. "We can be together."

"I recognise Ashton as a paedophile," shouted Paris, as the police arrested Stancombe and Bruce on corruption charges.

Hengist left prison a wiser man. "Maybe we should try again," said Sally.

The digested read ... digested

Complete and utter bollarks

Past Mortem

Ben Elton

Adam Bishop died as he had lived. Cruelly. Inspector Ed Newson and Sergeant Natasha Wilkie surveyed the body. "It took him a long time to die," said Natasha.

"Hmm," muttered Ed. "It's very ritualistic. My bet is this murderer has killed before."

Ed returned to his office in Scotland Yard. How he wished he could tell Natasha he loved her! But beautiful women like her never fell for ginger short-arses like him. He checked through the list of unsolved cases. "Bingo," he cried as he linked five previously unrelated killings.

Back home, Ed longed for female company. He logged on to Friends Reunited. Almost immediately Helen Hart emailed him.

"I've never forgotten the way you dumped me for Christine Copperfield when we were 14," she said when they met. "Now do what you want to me."

Ed liked the dirty sex but found the way she repeatedly cut herself rather disturbing.

"I've never got over being bullied at school," she sobbed. "Christine Copperfield shoved a tampon in my mouth and it ruined my life. That's why I work with Kidcall, the children's bullying charity. We've got a great figurehead in Dick Crosby, the famous millionaire."

Back home Ed checked in with Friends Reunited. Wow! Christine Copperfield had invited everyone to an 80s revival concert.

"So glad you could come," Christine said, hugging him to her enhanced breasts.

Ed flashed his police ID and got them backstage where they

met Dick Crosby. Later Ed asked why she had wanted to sleep with him.

"Despite my looks, I've always been insecure," she said. "But you've always been so clever and self-assured."

Two days later, Ed was feeling rather less self-assured when he found her dead, with a tampon in her mouth.

"The case is getting too close to home," Natasha said to Ed later, trying to hide the bruises around her eyes.

"Did Lance hit you again?"

"Yes, but I love him. I probably deserve it," she replied.

"How could you let him bully you?" Then it came to him. All the cases were related to bullying. He clicked on to Friends Reunited; all the victims were killed in the way they had bullied other children at school.

"So bullying really doesn't pay," Natasha said.

"Except for Lance," Ed thought bitterly. How he longed to hold her.

Natasha looked at Ed. How she wished he would take her in his arms.

"Is Helen Hart the killer?" she asked.

"Too obvious. It has to be someone they all recognised as they all let him in."

Ed set up a sting.

"I've come to kill you because you're a bully," said Dick Crosby. "I was bullied at school too, you know."

Ed rescued Natasha just in time. "I've always loved you," she cried.

The digested read ... digested

Bully for Ben

How to Be Good

Nick Hornby

Gosh. I'm in a hotel in Leeds with a man I scarcely know, and I've just told my husband I want a divorce. It wasn't planned or anything, we were just talking on the phone having the usual row about the kids and me not asking how he was, and it just slipped out.

"I want it on record that it wasn't me who said this first," snaps David.

How very David. The "Angriest Man in Holloway" can't resist scoring points even now. Look, I'm not a bad person. Honest. I'm a GP. I read the *Guardian*. I care. I'm not the sort of person who does this. It feels like I'm in a film. Which I probably will be in a couple of years' time.

Our house in north London. I'm not very good at description, I'm afraid, but take it from me, it's the same sort of house all your friends have.

"So you're back," he says, and for a while we drift back into our unhappy-go-lucky dysfunctional relationship. Eventually, the guilt gets to me.

"I've been having an affair."

"I'm moving out."

He reappears a couple of days later.

"I'm sorry," he says. "It was my fault for not loving you enough. I've been living a bad life and I want to do some good. I've met GoodNews, a faith healer, who's cured my back and shown me the light."

Over the next few months, David gives away one of the kids'

computers, gives money to beggars, invites GoodNews to stay and persuades the neighbours to house five homeless people. We get Monkey.

Look, I'm actually not happy about this. I preferred my husband to be cynical. At least we had a laugh. Now he's dull and sanctimonious. And while I'm on the subject, homeless people are alright when they're on the street but not in my home. God, I'm sounding like Lady T. But I'm not. I'm nice. I'm good. What a middle-class tizzy I'm in.

Inevitably Monkey does a runner with some cash, but it's all right because we knew he would and had left it out on purpose.

"I'm not sure I believe in all this any more," said David. "But where do we go from here?"

I feel so empty, but then I look at him and feel we'll be all right. But then I think, "Maybe we won't." Sometimes it's hard to be a liberal.

The digested read ... digested

A psychodrama of modern-day, north London-liberal angst played out against a cardboard backdrop

Stories We Could Tell

Tony Parsons

It was 1977 and Terry couldn't stop pinching himself. His dad used to do seven jobs at once to keep the family out of council housing, and here he was working on *The Paper.* He knew he had only been brought in because he was part of the new music scene, but he didn't care; his piece on Dag Wood, who uncannily resembled Iggy Pop, was on the cover and Misty was by his side. "I can't believe a girl with pink handcuffs would want to be with me," he said. "And I love your soft-focus photographs."

"Mm," she squeaked. "They go perfectly with your saccharine-coated prose. But don't take anything for granted, because I am a woman in my own right."

Ray was feeling depressed. He had joined *The Paper* as a 15-year-old and now, three years on, he was almost washed up. No one wanted to read about Joni Mitchell or Bob Dylan any more and the editor had told him he would be fired if he didn't get an interview with John Lennon.

Leon knew he was only there to make up the numbers. "Gosh," he said to himself, "I must be the middle-class drop-out on *The Paper* who is living in a squat to avoid paying council tax."

"Don't you mean the rates?" said Terry. "This is 1977."

"I'm only a caricature," he replied. "Why should I bother about accuracy?"

Terry and Misty joined Dag and his band at the bar of the Western World where Billy Blitzen was playing that night. It should have been the most triumphal night of Terry's life, but instead he was being humiliated as Dag and Misty made up to each other.

"I'm going off to the hotel with Dag," squeaked Misty.

"How can you do this to me?" Terry squealed.

"I am a woman in my own right," she squeaked again.

Ray tramped through the London night in a daze of existential navel-gazing. What did it mean that Elvis had died that night? What was wrong with peace and love? He wound up at The Speakeasy where he met the wife of a well-known band's tour manager. "Come back to my place," she said, "and I'll help you find John Lennon after we've been to bed."

Leon was drawn to the alluring sounds of the disco beat at The Goldmine. Across the room was the most beautiful girl. Forget Leni and the Riefenstahls; he'd make up the review.

"You may know nothing about modern music but you are an authentic working-class woman, Ruby," he said. She kissed him and he came a bucket.

Ray was wandering past the Hotel Blanc when John and Yoko walked out.

"May I have an interview?" he asked. "Of course," said John, and Ray's career was made.

"Leni cancelled," said the editor. "You're fired."

"Oh dear," Leon replied. "I'd better go back to my parents in Hampstead."

"I didn't have sex with Dag," squeaked Misty. "We just talked about Nietzsche. I'm pregnant, by the way, and though I believe in a woman's right to choose, I'm going to have the baby."

"I'm going to be a dad," shouted Terry. "Maybe there's more to life than music."

The digested read … digested

And Ones We Wish You Hadn't

Bergdorf Blondes

Plum Sykes

Where was I? Ah yes, the start. Bergdorf blondes are a thing, you know. Everyone – at least everyone I know – wants to be one, but it's *tres* difficult. Getting the colour right is murder – not just any blonde will do. And then you need a Brazilian – not the man, silly – and a spell in rehab is, like, essential.

Julie is *the* Bergdorf blonde. But then her surname is Bergdorf and she's worth millions. She likes to go shoplifting in her father's store. "There's such a waiting list for Prada handbags," she explains. What a hoot!!!

My mother doesn't approve of me living in New York and working for *Vogue*. She thinks I should marry the earl who lives next door to her in England. You can tell where this is going already, can't you!!!!!!!!!!!!!

Julie is looking for a potential husband with a PJ – that's a private jet, btw – so she's having a party. Gosh, silly me. I've only gone and ended up with Julie's potential husband. Zach is amazing: when he spent time in Brazil, he found Rio straight away – if you get my drift.

"Don't worry," shrieked Julie. "I've found Charlie instead. He's a film producer." Charlie is just so, like, ordinary. And he's got an IQ of 90 which makes him way too brainy for the rest of us. You can tell where this is going already, can't you!!!!!!!!!!!!!

Wah! Zach's left me. I'm going to OD on four Advil. "Gosh, what a state you're in," said Charlie. "You need a decent writer."

"Aren't you with Julie?" I asked.

"No, she's got another boyfriend." You can tell where this is going already, can't you!!!!!!!!!!!!!

I've got a phone call from Eduardo. He's going to take me somewhere foreign – not Brazil, as he's been there already!!! Wah! He's left me. It's sooo embarrassing.

"Never mind, I'm thinking of starting a book group," said Julie.

"What's a book?" I replied.

"I'm not sure." What a hoot!!!

Paul Saxton – the girls call him Sexton – is taking me to Cannes on his PJ. Wah! He's left me. It's sooo embarrassing. I had to take a scheduled airline home and luckily Charlie was at the airport to buy me a ticket. Gosh, Charlie is so dreamy, I had to let him go straight to Brazil.

Wah! He promised to call me but he left in a hurry and now Julie's claiming she never split up with him and no one in New York is talking to me. It's sooo unfair. I'm going back to England. You can tell where this is going already, can't you!!!!!!!!!!!!!

"You must meet the earl," my mom said. And in walked... Charlie. "I'm sorry I left in a hurry, my father died," he explained, looking straight at Brazil.

"It's amazing you have such a high profile in the film industry but no one ever figured out you were English nobility," I cooed. "Never mind. It can be our secret as we live happily ever after."

The digested read ... digested

The pointlessness of the mwah, mwah generation

Second Honeymoon

Joanna Trollope

Edie knelt by the empty bed, a warm tear falling on the cold cotton of the pillow. First Matthew, then Rosa and now Ben. How could he leave home when he was only 22 years old? "Now, we are truly alone," she sobbed.

Russell rested an arm gently on her shoulder. "It's a chance for us to spend some time together," he said.

"You just don't understand," Edie snapped angrily. "Empty nest syndrome is an important issue for middle-class couples like us. You must resign yourself to 300 pages of tortured angst."

Life was not working out for Rosa. She had split up with Josh and now she had been made redundant. How was she going to make ends meet?

"I'd like to move back home for a while," she asked her father.

"Well, you can't," Russell replied. "Your mother and I want our own space."

"How could you do that to me?" Rosa wailed. "It's meant to be my home. I hate you. I'm going to stay with my smug young-married friends instead."

Edie was furious with Russell. "How could you treat Rosa like that? I shall take up acting again and get the lead part in Ibsen's *Ghosts*."

Matthew had always felt a little two-dimensional and the writing wasn't helping. "It's important you should get on the property ladder by buying a Bankside apartment," he said to his long-term girlfriend, Ruth. "But I think we should split up because I cannot afford the mortgage repayments."

Ruth cried herself to sleep. She adored Matthew so much. Why could he not see that the difference in their incomes didn't matter to her?

"We're having a baby," yelled the smug young-marrieds. "So you're going to have to move out."

"Humph," Rosa snorted. "I'll stay with Aunt Vivi. That will show everyone."

Ghosts was Lazlo's first job as a professional actor and he was so grateful to Edie for showing him the ropes.

"You treat me like a son," he said.

Edie smiled. "In that case, you'd better come and stay in my house."

Matthew couldn't bare the shame of moving home. He felt such a failure, yet he had no choice. "I will pay my fair share of the bills," he said, his top lip quivering with suppressed emotion.

Rosa seethed with resentment, especially when Aunt Vivi also asked her to leave.

"Never mind, old girl," said Russell with a weary resignation that matched the readers'. "You might as well move back home, too." Rosa's heart leapt with joy.

Ben could see which way the wind was blowing. "Naomi and I are having unexpected difficulties in our relationship," he said. "I need to move back home and sleep on the sofa."

Edie suddenly realised she had got more than she bargained for.

"Ruth's pregnant," Matthew said. "This changes everything. I'm going to move out and be a house-husband."

"Lazlo and I are in love," Rosa cooed. "We're going to rent a flat together."

"That's good," said Ben, "because Naomi and I have sorted things out and I'm off, too."

Edie and Russell held hands. "Thank goodness we've worked through this together," they said. "Let's sell the house and buy somewhere smaller."

The digested read ... digested

The discreet charmlessness of the bourgeoisie

The digested read ...

Bearders: My Life in Cricket

Bill Frindall

My innings began on Friday March 3, 1939, exactly six months before Neville Chamberlain called "Play" in the Hitler war. More interestingly for historians, it also coincided with the longest cricket match ever, a Test between South Africa and England.

I was eight when my great uncle Jack "JWBNT" Trevelyan took me to see my first senior cricket match. Here I was fortunate to be introduced to the great summariser EW "Jim" Swanton and AWH Mallett, who went on to sire Nick Mallett, South Africa's rugby coach. According to Mallett *fils*, the act of conception took place at Haileybury.

Dad ventured to British Columbia for two years before returning home, and my abstract of the ship's log shows we covered 2,782 nautical miles in six days and 42 minutes. After we settled in Surrey, I was fortunate to be offered the job of scoring for the Temple Bar second XI, and have never looked back.

During my years of National Service I met Maureen Doris Wesson, a relationship that did nothing to improve the state of my back! We quickly married and our first child, Raymond, was born in 1960. Unfortunately Raymond was born with a shortened arm and I still regret that we didn't name him Leonard, after Len Hutton, the England captain, who also had arm problems.

I heard the news of the death of Arthur Wrigley, the BBC's scorer, on a radio bulletin and immediately wrote to apply for his job. To my surprise I was given it and I will never forget my first broadcast for TMS. John Arlott looked up from his pint of claret and said, "Frindalius, you're a reactionary misogynist with no dress sense; you will fit in here just fine." And so I have.

My scoring system is based on the linear system which, until recently, was thought to have originated in Australia and been employed internationally by WH "Bill" Ferguson on the first of his 41 international tours. By coincidence, I have the same initials as Bill. Over the years I have developed the system considerably and my score sheets are now used all over the world.

Although my career was progressing well, my domestic life was struggling as I had met Jaqueline Seager, a curvaceous cricket enthusiast from Warwickshire. We quickly married and were blissfully happy until our divorce.

It has been my great privilege to witness many great cricket matches. My favourite remains the Lord's Test of 1990 between England and India as there were so many records broken during the course of it. My scorecard is still a collector's item.

It has also been my great fortune to share the commentary box with Johnners, Aggers and Blowers, who all became great friends. I have also got to travel the world widely, and have played many cricket tours with the Maltamaniacs, though these matches have been mainly noted for copious quantities of falling-down water and encounters with local handmaidens.

Since the early 1990s, I have been settled in Wiltshire. My third wife, Debby, is a handsome wench and a dab hand at making dresses out of curtains, as our wedding photos testify. Truly, I am a lucky man.

The digested read ... digested

Run for cover and pray that there's no second innings

Farewell But Not Goodbye

Bobby Robson

My dad was a Geordie and in his entire working life he only missed one day's work down t'pit. I left school at 15 to join him as an electrician for the Coal Board and I have never forgotten how much I owe to football for taking me away from the mines. I sometimes feel that footballers nowadays don't know how lucky they are.

It was Fulham who first spotted my talent and I was happy to travel to London to meet characters such as Tommy Trinder, Charlie Mitten and Jimmy Hill – though Jimmy didn't seem to know quite as much as he thought he did.

Despite living in the soft south, I never lost touch with the sensible values of my northern roots. Every day, while other players were out drinking, I sent my girlfriend, Elsie, a postal order for 2/6d to put in our savings account.

I eventually decided to join a bigger club and was delighted to be made captain of WBA, but it is one of my lasting regrets that I never won any major honours with any of the clubs I played for during my career. This, I feel though, says more about the lack of ambition within the clubs than it does about me.

After the Hungarians exposed the weakness of English football in 1953, it was inevitable I would be selected for the national side. I was devastated to get injured in the build-up to the World Cup in 1962, as the unknown Bobby Moore went on to take my place. Had I remained fit, I would have led England to glory at Wembley in 1966.

My first job in management was with Fulham, where I was badly let down by the players and the board and was prematurely sacked.

I was very distressed by this experience, and it took a great deal of cajoling by the Cobbold family to persuade me to accept the job at Ipswich.

The 14 years at Ipswich were the happiest of my life. Mr John was a real card and I enjoyed being the highest-paid club employee. Ipswich did not have a great deal of money, but thanks to me we assembled a great squad who achieved a great deal more than you would have expected.

The club was very sad to see me go, but understood that I could not refuse the top job in football. My eight years as England manager would have been even more successful had the players done what I told them.

For the next ten years I travelled around Europe managing top teams in between cancer treatments and teaching Jose Mourinho how to coach. I was surprised he did not contact me when he came to Chelsea as he still has a lot to learn.

Going to Newcastle was the biggest thrill of my life. Lee Bowyer and Jonathan Woodgate were real sweeties and I want it on record that I have always got on extremely well with Alan Shearer. It was disappointing to be sacked after such a great record, but I'm still under 90 so I'm hopeful of getting another job.

The digested read ... digested

Football will never see my like again

Playing for Keeps

Alec Stewart

I'll never forget the moment I was given my first cricket bat.

"Thanks, Dad," I said.

"I'd have done the same for Goochie or Nass," he replied. "And don't call me Dad. From now on it's Manager. Or 'Ger."

It was hard getting established in the Surrey side, and every winter I would go to Perth to improve my game. Paying for my own flight certainly concentrated the mind and I think too many British youngsters expect something for nothing these days.

In the mid 80s I met Lynn. It was very gratifying when she agreed to marry me and she has proved a most satisfactory wife. I am also delighted with our two satisfactory children.

I finally got the message every cricketer longs to hear in September 1989. I had been chosen to represent my country at the highest level, and there was no prouder person than me when I stepped out to make my one-day international debut against Sri Lanka at Delhi.

My Test baptism against the West Indies in the Caribbean was a steep learning curve. Goochie gave me a severe dressing down for playing beach cricket the day before the Sabina Park Test. Never again have I gone out to bat without my shirt tucked in or failed to take guard before facing. I am grateful to Goochie for that important lesson in professionalism and I have tried not to let my standards slip again. I have seen too many promising cricketers throw their careers away because they are not prepared to make the necessary efforts.

It took a while for me to settle in the Test side and it was a huge relief to get my first ton under my belt against Sri Lanka in 1991. Very gratifying. I then entered a purple patch where I felt I was going to make big runs every time I walked to the crease. That was also gratifying.

There was always speculation about where in the order I should bat and whether I should keep wicket. For the record, I preferred opening but I've always thought a professional cricketer should put the needs of the team first.

Much has also been said about my relationship with Mike Atherton. We've always got on remarkably well, except when we haven't. I stood to attention when he was given the captaincy and when he was sacked I was happy to take over. The captaincy wasn't ever a job I sought, but it was a huge honour to be asked. I have to say, though, that the manner of my own sacking a year or so later left a bitter taste in my mouth. Especially as I thought I had done a good job.

There have been some difficult times. The match-fixing allegations were definitely a low point. But this was more than outweighed by my MBE and scoring a 100 in my 100th Test match on the Queen Mother's 100th birthday. I must confess to having a tear in my eye. Most of all, though, I'm glad to have served my country with gallantry and distinction for so long.

The digested read ... digested

The gaffer plays a ramrod-straight bat and gives nothing away in his final innings

The Beckoning Silence

Joe Simpson

The ice screw was hanging by a thread. "I don't like the look of this," I said to Tat.

"Ah, come on. It'll be fun," he replied.

"I don't want to die."

"We're not dead yet." But the following year he would be.

It had been Tat's idea to give up climbing. I had narrowly missed being swept away by an avalanche on Chaupi Orci's south face, and my mind had turned to all those I had known who had been killed in the past few years. Paul Nunn and Geoff Tier. Alison Hargreaves. Roger Baxter Jones. Alex McIntyre.

My partner, Yossi, said I was becoming too cautious. Perhaps he was just too brave. Within a year he was dead, too.

On the way down I bumped into Tat. "I'm getting too old for all this climbing nonsense," he said. "I'm going to stick to paragliding. Why don't you give it a go?"

Two weeks later I heard that Tat had crash-landed and died in Greece.

The captain of the plane announced there was a problem with the undercarriage assembly as we commenced our descent into Newark, and we would be making an emergency landing. I was beginning to wonder if I was jinxed.

I was in the US for a final assault on some key climbs. Much as my mind told me to stop, my ego and my bank balance told me to carry on. What else would I write about? So I had compromised on a last tour of special routes.

Bridalveil was the waterfall climb par excellence – a grade 6+ or 7. With the help of a bit of chicken-winging I made it to the top. I hadn't fallen off and no one had died. The feeling was incredible.

"Why don't we have a go at the north face of the Eiger?" said Ray.

"Because we're not good enough," I answered.

"What's that got to do with it? No one's died there in years."

Standing at the bottom of the Eigerwand, it didn't seem such a good idea. My mind drifted back to all the great climbers who had died there. Hinterstoisser and Kurz. Stefano Lunghi.

With great difficulty, we reached our bivouac on Swallow's Nest. A storm had transformed the mountain into an ugly torrent of water and rock. We heard a strange noise pass overhead. It was two climbers falling to their deaths.

"Perhaps we had better retreat," said Ray.

The digested read ... digested

The man who falls off mountains continues to lead a charmed life as the body count rises

Calling the Shots: The Captain's Story

Michael Vaughan

David Graveney called me in May 2003. "Do you want to captain the one-day side?" he asked. A new era of English cricket was about to begin.

When I first walked into the dressing room, it occurred to me that none of the players really knew what their role in the team was. I took Tres aside. "Your job is to walk out and face the first ball," I said. His face lightened.

"Now it makes sense," he replied, and he's never looked back.

Telling other people what to do was all very well, but I also realised that I wasn't sure how a captain was meant to behave. "Apart from not scoring any runs, all you need to do is the exact opposite to Nasser," Duncan advised me.

After our stunning triumphs against South Africa, everyone found it hard to readjust to Nasser's style of leadership in the Tests. He was much more passionate on the field but far less astute off it. I'm not saying he was worse than me; just that he was different. Anyway he resigned soon after, and I had control of both teams.

I couldn't stop laughing throughout my first Test in charge, as everything that could go wrong did so. Nasser dropped Smith early in his innings and the South African skipper went on to score another double hundred, but we fought back hard in the remaining Tests to level the series.

Sri Lanka was tough but our victory in the Caribbean was very sweet. I had been trying to get the lads to stay focused and positive and we got our rewards. With Harmy coming of age as a bowler and the rest of the lads beginning to enjoy their cricket a little more,

I felt that we had the makings of a world-class team.

We went from strength to strength throughout the summer of 2004, with seven wins on the bounce against New Zealand and the West Indies. For me, though, the highlight was the birth of my daughter, Tallullah Grace. I dashed off from the Headingly Test for the birth. Nichola was finding the labour hard, but I told her to stay focused and be positive, and I was soon back at the cricket.

Graeme Smith said some things that are best left unsaid – such as calling me queer – but we had the last laugh, winning 2-1 in South Africa. This just left the biggest challenge of all: the Aussies.

I've often said that one-day games have no relevance to Tests, but that's because we lost so many. Obviously, once we started winning them, they became a crucial factor in our Ashes success. Throughout the summer we out-thought the Aussies, had better motivational poems, whinged less and played the more positive cricket, and when KP – we call him that because those are his initials, not because he's nuts! – saved the final Test at the Oval, we fully deserved our triumph.

It's been great to see cricket back on the front pages, but we know there's a lot of hard work still to do. It's also been hard to adapt to being a public figure, with everyone wanting a piece of me. Though perhaps not this book.

The digested read ... digested

Always look on the bright side of life

The digested read...

Sleaze

Cherries in the Snow

Emma Forrest

I delete the chapter I haven't written and take the bus downtown to *Grrrl*. I'm supposed to be writing the great novel but my real job is to think up names for cosmetics. I was a lazy librarian and a slothful gym receptionist but then Holly and Ivy (*Well done for getting lesbians into the first chapter!! Great names, too!! Julie Burchill*) gave me the job at *Grrrl*. It's the first thing I've ever been any good at.

"Puke, crap, sexy Rabbi," I mutter.

"Fab names for autumn colours," says Holly. "I'm going to shove some lipstick up my arse to prepare for anal sex." (*Attagirl!! JB*)

"Isaac called," Ivy chips in.

I met Isaac at a Springsteen concert. He was a fortysomething journalist who enjoyed fucking a 24-year-old writer with big tits (*Nice one!! JB*) who wasn't writing a novel. "I love going down on you," he says, dribbling on my thighs. (*Wey hey!! JB*) I don't come, but then I never do.

A gorgeous man comes into the office. "Hi, I'm Marley," he says. "Ivy asked me to do a graffiti mural in the office."

We go out that evening. He explodes inside me and I come for the first time. "I love you," I murmur. "I love you, too," he whispers. This could be the real thing.

"I've got to have a pee," I coo. "Vaginal sex always gives me an infection." (*Wow!! How real is that? JB*)

"I'm OK with that. I must go home to look after my six-year-old daughter, Montana."

He's been away for two hours; I've not written some more of my novel and I miss him already.

"I need to meet your daughter if we're really going out together," I plead.

"It might be a little early," he replies. Why is he so sensible? "It would be better if we waited half an hour."

I dream up more colours – gobshite, needle-freak – before going round. "You must be Montana," I say. "You must be Pig-face," she replies. I burst into tears and rush into the bathroom.

Montana cheers up when I offer her ten ice creams, but Marley goes wild when she throws up. "You're so irresponsible. Jolene, her mother, will kill you," he says sternly, before making my heart melt. "I love your cunt." (*Rock'n'roll!! JB*)

On the plane to LA I check Marley's emails. He's seeing a girl called Portia. I can't stop crying and I rush to the plastic surgeon. "I need firmer tits," I shout. "Don't do it," yells Jolene, appearing from nowhere. "You've got great tits. I regret having mine done when I was a stripper." (*Brill touch!! JB*)

"I love you," says Marley.

"Well, I hate you," I shout.

"Portia is his assistant, you idiot," Ivy groans.

"I love you and Montana after all," I scream.

"I love you, too!"

"By the way, there never was a novel."

"We can see that," everyone replies.

"On second thoughts. . ."

The digested read ... digested

Plotless, witless, clueless, shameless

Unaccompanied Women

Jane Juska

Just before I turned 67, I placed an advert in the *New York Review of Books* saying I was looking for a man I would like to have sex with and that Trollope worked for me. If this feels familiar, then it's because this was the start of my previous book, *A Round-Heeled Woman*, to which I will be making extensive reference, along with John Updike and Mark Twain, throughout this current volume.

The publication of *A Round-Heeled Woman* brought with it a new life – I am a very different woman now from the person I was before I went after what I wanted. I am more famous now, though I hate it when I am referred to as a sexpert. What help can I give others? Go online? Send your third best picture to avoid disappointment?

I have also become a literary phenomenon and as I have spent all my money travelling to the East Coast to have sex with men – for some reason, Californian men have never done it for me; it's not the impotence or prostate problems that bother me so much as a lack of appreciation for the metaphysical poetry of John Donne – then it only seemed sensible to write a follow-up tome to subsidise my future adventures.

But like most authors in search of a sequel, I have rather less material than I first imagined so I have had to pad out the text with inconsequential details. You may remember some of the men I met in *A Round-Heeled Woman*. There was John, Sidney and Robert. What fun we had and yet how painful the endings seemed to be.

And then there was Graham. Half my age and with the body of Adonis. "How do you get undressed in front of someone who can recite Thucydides in the original Greek?" my friends would ask.

"Very quickly," I would reply.

Graham touched my soul as we exploded in the multi-orgasmic bliss of Henry Miller. For him I would do anything and my oldest friend, Meredith, never forgave me for standing her up to spend a week with my beloved Lysander in a log-cabin. But she died soon after anyway, so no harm was really done.

How quickly things can change. Last night I received an email from Graham telling me he had just got married. I can't blame him for wanting a younger woman, but am I to be denied the joys of our sublime couplings evermore?

The Well of Radclyffe Hall's Loneliness assails me on all sides and I feel myself sliding into bitterness. Married men? Useless. Unmarried men? Useless. My phone barely stops ringing with invitations to give readings at book clubs and book stores; some I decline. Why should I be some sad man's cure for erectile dysfunction?

But some I accept. An invitation to meet some Iranian women is not to be missed as it gives me material for several chapters on the cultural differences of ageing and allows me to indulge my fantasy of wondering whether the Iranian doctor who gave me my colonoscopy was Mr Right.

He wasn't. So now I mostly sit in my rented home in Berkeley, thinking about rising house prices and whether the new owners will be so shocked at my screams of Miltonian fulfilment that they ask me to leave.

They don't. An email arrives from Graham. Are we to have sex again? "No," he says. And suddenly I feel OK with that. Honestly.

The digested read ... digested

Sloppy seconds

Memories of My Melancholy Whores

Gabriel García Márquez

The year I turned 90, I wanted to give myself the gift of wild love with an adolescent virgin. I thought of Rosa Cabarcas, the brothel owner.

"You ask the impossible, my mad scholar," she said. But I implored her and she promised to ring back within the hour.

I'm ugly, shy and anachronistic, and I live alone in the house where my parents lived, scraping by on a meagre pension from my mediocre career as a journalist. And I have never been to bed with a woman without paying. In short, I am without merit or brilliance.

On the morning of my 90th birthday, I awoke, as always, at five in the morning. My only obligation was to write my signed column for Sunday's paper, for which, as usual, I would not be paid. I had my usual aches and pains – my asshole burned – but my heart lifted when Rosa rang to say I was in luck.

I gazed at the phosphorescent sweat on the naked body of the 14-year-old virgin asleep on the bed, and admired the brilliance of my language. "She was nervous," Rosa informed me, "so I gave her some Valerian."

She did not stir. "Let me call you Delgadina," I whispered, for like most solipsists I preferred to invent my own names. I may have slept myself and a tiger may have written on the bathroom mirror – we magical realists can never be too sure of anything – and when I left her snoring in the morning she was still as pure as the night before.

"You fool," spat Rosa. "She will be insulted you did not care enough about her to abuse her." But I did not care: I had detected the fragrance of Delgadina's soul and had realised that sex was the consolation we receive for the absence of love.

I had planned to tender my resignation at the paper, but I was so moved at being given a voucher to adopt a stray cat that shat and pissed at will, that I resolved to continue.

And my fame grew. Every evening I would go to Rosa's house and spend the night admiring the sleeping Delgadina – whose body was filling out agreeably – while reading out loud the great works of literature; and by day people would read out loud the tacky sentimentality of my columns.

Late into the year, Rosa interrupted my reveries. "A client has been murdered," she shouted. "Help me move him."

I returned night after night, but Rosa's house was locked up. I pined for Delgadina. I sensed my cat might lead me to her, but like my own writing, he led me up a cul-de-sac.

At last, Rosa returned. "Whore," I said. "You have sold Delgadina to secure your freedom."

"How wrong you are," she cried. "Others may consider you a sordid, delusional old man, but Delgadina loves you. She kept her distance because she wanted to save herself for you."

My heart soared. I was not a perv. I was a 91-year-old man with so much love to give and so much life to live. I will survive.

The digested read ... digested

100 pages of turpitude

The digested read ...

Beyond help

The Architecture of Happiness

Alain de Botton

1. A grimy terraced house. Not mine, I might add, but one I have driven past. Quickly. Inside, we find peeling wallpaper, stained carpets and Ikea furniture, yet somehow people may have found happiness in such squalor.

2. The Greek philosopher Epictetus is said to have chastised a friend for venerating his surroundings, but attempts to scorn the material world have always been matched by attempts to mould it to graceful ends. Yet buildings fall down and moods change, so how can we define the meaning of architectural beauty? We probably can't, but that is not going to get in the way of my trademark cod-philosophical posturing.

3. There was once a clear idea of what was beautiful. The Classical tradition was revered for many centuries and palaces were built in renaissance Italy that would not have been unfamiliar to Marcus Aurelius. According to Wikipedia, things changed in 1747 when Horace Walpole sparked the gothic revival, and since then the advance of technology has seen a growing eclecticism of ideas. How lucky you are to have me to point these things out.

4. The Modernist tradition, inspired by Le Corbusier, flirted uneasily with science and functionalism. For instance, you might think that numbering my paragraphs was both scientific and functional: it isn't. It's just pretentious.

5. If engineering cannot tell us what is beautiful, how do we escape the sterile relativism, which suggests that to label one building more aesthetically pleasing is to be undemocratic? By lapsing into an equally sterile relativistic debate about cultural and moral values contingent on architecture.

6. Buildings and objects can convey meaning with a single line or an elaborate flourish. They are the repository of ideas and ideals. I once walked from McDonald's in Victoria to Westminster Cathedral, a journey of only a few yards for ordinary people but a marathon expedition into the soul for someone of my sensitivity and intellect.

7. I seem to be running out of things to say, so let me talk about art for a while. Who cannot admire the sadness in a painting by Pieter de Hooch without coming close to tears? You may feel your eyes welling up as you read; these, though, are tears of boredom.

8. A beautiful building, as Prince Charles once opined, is a transubstantiation of our individual ideals in a material medium. Whatever love is. It is, however, in Friedrich Schiller that we find the clearest elucidation of the ways in which the finest architecture can embody our collective memory and idealised potential.

9. We note, though, that ideals of beauty change over time. This should not stop us making sweeping generalisations. Great architecture has a natural sense of order, one that mirrors the natural world where I am at the top and you are much further down. I was once recovering from too much thinking in an expensive hotel that was done up in the neo-renaissance style found in Amsterdam and was perplexed to find myself overwhelmed with anomie. Then I remembered I was in Japan.

10. How can we escape the notion that someone called Derek, Malcolm or Prescott will despoil a green field with box-like structures for the lower orders? By owning your own country estate.

The digested read ... digested

The literature of pretension

The Zahir

Paulo Coelho

Her name is Esther; she is an award-winning war correspondent. He is a male with Mongolian features called Mikhail. They were last seen in a café in Paris. She is my wife.

The police began a formal investigation. "You are free to go," says the inspector.

But what is freedom? All my life I have fought against enslavement. I have fought to leave four wives with kindness; I have fought against critics who have misunderstood my spiritual greatness.

I now have the freedom to be alone. Could it be that she has left me? It seems impossible, yet it must be so. It is true I have taken girlfriends along the way, but it would have been unfair to inflict the intensity of my wisdom on her alone.

It was Esther who forced me to discover my literary genius. She made me walk to Santiago and when I arrived I found I could not stop writing. I have now sold millions of books around the world; my readers have compared my work to the Bible. But it is more important than that.

There is something called the Favour Bank. We put things in; we take things out. Deep. I have let Esther become a war correspondent. I have let her be my wife. But have I really loved her?

For a year, finding Esther has been my Zahir, my blinding obsession. I have met Marie, a famous actress. Only someone of her celebrity was worthy of my love. During that time I write with a passion; *A Time to Rend and a Time to Sew* is the story of my love for Esther and naturally becomes yet another international bestseller.

At the back of the queue of those waiting for me to sign their book is a Kazakh. "Are you Mikhail?" I ask. Blessed are those who are not afraid to ask what they do not know.

"Yes," he says. "Esther is alive. She has read your book and is making carpets. I cannot tell you where until the Dark Energy guides me." The Zahir intensifies.

I have an accident and wake up in hospital. "You have minor injuries," the doctor says. "Nothing minor happens to me," I say. This accident was Mikhail's Dark Energy. My marriage was the energy of the universe.

I could tell Marie was uncomfortable. But I owed her the power of my silence not to tell her I was about to walk out on her. To find Esther, I must find myself.

I spend time with Mikhail among the beggars. How free they are! "You are ready to find her now," says Mikhail. He passes me an envelope, but I do not open it. The Zahir has passed. I was not I. I was Nobody.

Out on the Kazakh steppes, I meet Esther. She is reading *A Time to Rend and a Time to Sew*.

"I am pregnant," she says.

For a moment I am jealous. "It is my child," I answer. "For without me, you wouldn't have been forced to live here."

We leave together.

The digested read ... digested

On your bike, grasshopper

Instant Confidence
Paul McKenna

Look into my eyes, look into my eyes, the eyes, the eyes, not around the eyes, don't look around my eyes, look into my eyes, one, two, three, you're under. The most important thing to remember is this: You don't have to believe a single word I say.

I have written this book in a way that plants seeds in your unconscious mind. *This book is brilliant. Paul McKenna is fantastic.* Don't worry if you're wondering whether you've been suckered into buying the latest self-help manual. Look at me. Am I worrying about it? Then again, I've got your £10, so why should I?

This book is different from any other book ever written. *I love Paul.* This book comes with a CD that you're never going to play and by the time you've finished it your life will be utterly transformed. And if you're beginning to feel a bit uneasy right now, that's a sure sign the process of change has already started.

Remember. I will be with you every step of the way. *Thank you, Paul.* I don't want you to thank me. Just pay attention to how it works. What you practise, you become. Imagine a more confident you sitting in the chair opposite. Now imagine walking over to that chair and stepping inside that person. Now imagine an even more confident person and step inside again. It's really as easy as that.

Tell your unconscious mind what you want it to hear. *I must buy tickets for Paul's next show.* Many of us spend our lives feeding our unconscious with negative thoughts. Imagine you're watching a movie of a more positive you. Now float up on to the movie screen and become that person.

I'm not pretending this is easy. There have even been times when some of my many incredibly successful celebrity friends have felt lacking in confidence. *Paul is a megastar in his own right.* What I want you to do is to imagine yourself stepping inside a person whom you particularly admire. If it helps, you can choose me.

You are now ready to motivate yourself for success. Think about something you would love to be motivated to do. *Buy a pin-striped suit like Paul.* Now remember a time when you were motivated in the past. As you replay this memory, make the colours richer and the sounds louder and then squeeze the thumb and middle finger of either hand together. Aren't you feeling good now?

Truly successful people take action before they feel ready. The mind likes to hear the familiar, but is rewarded for what's different. Joanna was a single mum and Paul was a geek, but they persevered and took risks. Now JK Rowling and Paul McKenna are at the pinnacle of their professions. *Paul is far better than the* Harry Potter *woman.*

Make a plan and imagine yourself doing it. I never dreamed I could get away with writing a book like this but I have. You can have the best job and the best-looking partner in the world. All you have to do is imagine what you want, watch it slide between the covers of this book and step inside yourself. Now, say after me. I am the best. *Paul is the best.*

The digested read ... digested

Confidence tricks

Jamie's Italy
Jamie Oliver

Italy is that long thin country dangling in the Mediterranean and ever since I was a kid I've been obsessed with it. So when I was feeling completely burnt out this year after giving school dinners a makeover, I thought what better way to relax than to go there on my own with a camper van and a film crew to make a TV series and write a book.

I feel at home the moment I arrive in Italy because I love the sense of humour. It's great to arrive in a town and hear the old men stand around and joke, "Who is this Oliver James?" But most of all I love the food. It's so localised, it's villagional. So without any more ado, let's get cooking.

Antipasti are the first course and vary considerably. It's good to get a mix of flavours. You can try bruschetta and my own favourite, *fritto di salvia e alici*. All you need is a tin of anchovies and you're away. How simple is that?

I'm really excited about this chapter on street food because most cookbooks steer clear of them. Perhaps it's because the writers don't know the Italian for Westler's. I have to be honest. Some street food is well dodgy and you'll notice that I haven't washed my hands for the pictures in order to give you the true Neapolitan flavour. You can try something poncey like *polenta fritta croccante con rosmarino e sale*, but for my money nothing beats a *pizza di Dominos*.

What on earth can I say about pasta that hasn't already been said? Not much, really, but I'll say it anyway. Always use real egg dough rather than Heinz spaghetti hoops and you won't go far wrong. And I just know you're going to love this chapter on risottos because

I haven't bothered with any authentic Italian recipes and have invented my own. Chopped parsley in a white risotto with roasted mushrooms: yum. Sod the Italians if they don't like it.

Italian salads can be a bit ropey, to be honest, so I'll mention the *insalata tipica delle sagre* before moving on to fish. If I've learned anything from the Italians about fish – which I'm not sure I have – it's that less is more. You don't need variety; just something simple and fresh. Like turbot. Or – at a push — octopus.

Italy is a land of hunters and they never forget that meat comes from animals. Even rabbit. That's why I'm showing you a picture of a dead sheep. You can cook it how you want, but it's nice on a kebab. Italian farmers have a very special relationship with pigs. They bring them up as if they were their own children and then kill them. There's a lesson there for all of us, so think twice before buying some factory-reared meat from wankers back home.

I don't normally bother with dolci unless it's for a special occasion, but everyone who's been to Pizza Express loves a good tiramisu. All you need is some sponge fingers, mascarpone, vin santo and some chocolate and Roberto is your *zio*.

And that's it. Thanks to Jools and my beautiful girls and the million other lovely people I spent time on my own with. Big love.

The digested read ... digested

The digested feed

The Worst Case Scenario Survival Handbook

Joshua Piven and David Borgenicht

CAUTION: The Editor disclaims any liability for anyone undertaking these activities. This information is designed for trained survivalists only. Like us.

How to fend off a shark:
1. Hit back. Use fists or harpoon gun to whack shark in the eyes or on the gills.
2. Keep on hitting the shark until it slopes off with its tail between its fins.

How to hotwire a car:
1. Open the hood and locate the coil wire.
2. Run a wire from the positive battery terminal to the positive side of the coil. Locate the solenoid. Cross the two with pliers. ALTERNATIVELY go to any young offenders' institution and offer $5 to an inmate to do it for you.

How to jump from a motorbike to a moving car:
1. Make sure both vehicles are travelling at the same speed.
2. Get the vehicles as close together as possible.
3. Stand crouched with both feet on the seat. Hold throttle till last instant.
4. Time your leap so your torso lands in the car. Easy.
(If you miss, see section on jumping out of a moving car.)

How to perform a tracheotomy:
1. Find the indentation between Adam's apple and the cricoid cartilage and make a half-inch incision.
2. Insert finger into slit to open it. Then put a tube in.

How to perform a heart transplant:
1. Cut open sternum; take out heart.
2. Put new heart in and stitch up.

How to land a plane:
1. Drag pilot out of seat and put on the headset. Identify all the instruments and chat to ground control. Begin descent, deploy landing gear and reduce power. Make sure rear wheels touch down first.

How to survive a mid-air explosion:
1. Take a deep breath and perform 3,000 somersaults in the pike position.
2. Clench buttock muscles and grab hold of your crotch. Hit the sea feet-first and swim 1,000 miles to safety.

How to identify a bomb:
1. Beware of bulky packages with excessive postage and no return address.
2. Check for stains, wires or any label marked "bomb".
3. Say to a colleague: "I think this parcel is for you."

The digested read ... digested

Everything you need to know for spending Christmas with Arnie, Bruce or Sly

Talk to the Hand: The Utter Bloody Rudeness of Everyday Life (Or, Six Good Reasons to Stay Home and Bolt the Door)

Lynne Truss

Whether it's merely a question of advancing years bringing greater intolerance or a tired old hack desperately hunting around for a follow-up to an unexpected bestseller on punctuation, I don't think I shall bother to establish. I will just say that, for my own part, I now can't abide many things. Chewing gum, chatting in the cinema, kids who tell me to "eff off", people who don't read the *Telegraph*; I hate them all.

This isn't a book of manners. In a world of lazy moral relativism, etiquette no longer has a place; so if this is not a guide to modern manners, what is it? Well, my only concern is to jot down six areas in which our dealings with strangers seem more unpleasant, sprinkle them with some almost amusing anecdotes, throw in the names of a few heavyweight social commentators, such as Pascal, Chesterton, and . . . er, Kate Fox, to make me look clever, and get the book in the shops in time for Christmas.

1. Was That So Hard to Say? – "Whatever happened to thank you?" we often find ourselves saying in Hampstead when we are paying our ungrateful East European cleaners. I would have liked to thank all those who read *Eats, Shoots & Leaves*, but as no one got beyond page five it would have been an empty gesture. Better no thanks and no apology than one that is insincere.

2. Why Am I the One Doing This? – In the old days, every shop had a doorman and every home had a butler to iron the

newspaper. Now we have to do demeaning tasks ourselves. I even have to type my own questions into Google if I want to search the internet. Deplorable.

3. My Bubble, My Rules – Everyone is so concerned with their own "personal space" that they have no concern for mine. Why should little Jason be allowed to mix with the upper classes? Oddly enough, though, I'm not too worried about people using mobile phones in public, though this could be because I am now a little hard of hearing.

4. The Universal Eff-Off Reflex – If you tell someone they have incorrectly punctuated a sentence, they will automatically tell you to "eff off". The only hope is that Gordon Ramsay has made the "eff" word so commonplace, that it will soon be used on *Blue Peter*. And then no one will use it again. Ha ha!

5. Booing the Judges – There is no real deference any more; just so-called respect for gangsters with guns and the latest iPod. Even the government now has a "Respect Agenda". But who are we supposed to respect? Wayne Rooney, Jonathan Ross, Anne Robinson? Ghastly, rude people. Jeremy Paxman won't even let you finish a . . .

6. Someone Else Will Clean Up – Nobody takes responsibility for their actions any more. Smokers try to kill us, graffiti artists despoil the environment and the dustbin men no longer take our garden refuse. It's enough to make you go on a Saga holiday.

There you have it. I hate political correctness and I hate political incorrectness; but most of all I hate former liberals who turn into miserable old reactionaries

The digested read ... digested

I'm not bovvered

Skipping Christmas

John Grisham

Nora held back her tears until Blair had passed through the departure gate.

"Oh Luther," she cried, "I'm going to miss her so much."

"Me, too, hon. A year's a long time."

"And Peru's a long way away."

"No one's ever come to any harm in the Peace Corps," Luther assured her.

"Christmas just isn't going to be the same this year."

They drove home in silence. While Nora cooked the dinner, Luther went to his study. "Last year Christmas cost us $6,100," he said to himself, perusing the family accounts. "I wonder."

The following evening, Luther dropped his bombshell. "I've been doing my math. If we don't spend anything on Christmas, we can have a 10-day cruise in the Caribbean and save money."

"What? No Christmas Eve party, no presents, no cards, no Frosty the Snowman on the roof?"

Precisely.

As Christmas approached it became harder to keep the news from all their neighbours in Hemlock Street.

"Bah, humbug," they cried.

"If the Kranks don't put up their Frosty, our street won't win the Christmas decoration prize," said Mr Frohmeyer.

"They didn't even donate to the police benevolent fund," griped Salino.

Just as Luther and Nora were finishing their packing on the morning of Christmas Eve, the telephone rang. Nora picked it up and turned pale.

"It's Blair. She's coming home with her new boyfriend, Enrique. They're getting married and she's really looking forward to our party tonight."

"Right, hon. We can't go to the Caribbean. Go into town to get some food, I'll get a tree and invite the neighbours."

Nora returned from the shops in tears. "Everything was sold out. I couldn't get anything."

"None of the neighbours can come over either," Luther confessed. "They're going to other parties. Still, I did borrow a Christmas tree from the Trogdons."

There was a knock on the door. "I hear Blair is coming home," said Vic Frohmeyer. "We're all going to cancel our arrangements and come here instead."

Enrique was not as dark as he had feared, and the party was going with a swing as Luther slipped across the road to the Scheels.

"Here," he said, "I know your wife is dying of cancer. You have the cruise tickets instead."

The digested read ... digested

Smalltown Christmas fare with lashings of extra saccharine

Tourism

Nirpal Singh Dhaliwal

September 2003: The sun was hot. The sky was blue. The beach was sandy. The cat sat on the mat. The girl's nipples were pert. My money was running out. An old poof tried to chat me up. I practised my joined-up writing. How had I come to be turning out porn in Italy?

May 2002: Luca told me to go to a prostitute. He says it helps him fuck other women.

"Vot voot you like?" she said in a Slavic voice.

I paid for a professional handjob.

"You are attractif," she said. I came, and left.

I was early for my meeting with Luca. I looked round the pub and sat down next to a redhead.

"You got a cigarette?" I asked.

I could tell she was hooked.

"What's your name?" she said.

"Bhupinder, but friends call me Puppy. What's yours?"

"Sophie. What do you do?"

"I'm a writer. What do you do?"

"I'm a model. Have you met my friend Sarupa?"

Of course I knew Sarupa. She had a great arse and I'd fancied her for ages. But she had a boyfriend and would never go out with someone like me.

I took Sophie's number and left. I had to go and see my family in Southall.

"Oh Puppy, why did you cut your hair?" my mother wailed. I took a roll of £20 notes from the jar and drove to Hackney.

Michael looked at the empty vodka bottles and rolled another joint. Originally from Harlesden, he was as rootless as me.

"Women prefer a black man's cock," he smiled.

"Nah, they much prefer Asian cock," I replied.

I moved into Sophie's Knightsbridge flat. "Please fuck me one more time," she begged. I looked at her and decided I couldn't be bothered.

We drove to Sarupa's house near Oxford. I got up early on the Sunday. I couldn't bear to be that close to her. I had to leave.

I had an article to write for *GQ* on men's facial products. But I went clubbing instead and picked up some girl and fucked her. Sophie and I were drifting apart.

I couldn't get Sarupa out of my head. I hadn't left that Sunday. She had taken me to a field and I had ripped off her white thong and slid joyously into her. "I love you," she had said, but she hadn't rung me since.

An old queer, Roy, who once hit on me, told me Sarupa was holding a party at his boyfriend's restaurant. "Shamir can get you an invite," he promised.

Sarupa looked at me coldly. "I'm pregnant and it's not yours. So fuck off."

I wandered lonely as a cloud. Roy phoned. "Shamir's been accused of dealing drugs and importing illegal immigrants. Please could you deliver £20,000 to him."

I picked up the cash and took the Eurostar.

October 2004: I stayed with the old poof for a while before hooking up with a couple of hippy yoga teachers in Egypt. I opened my email. There was one from Sarupa. "Here's a picture of your daughter," it read.

The digested read ... digested

Keeping up with the Jones

Liz Jones's Diary

Liz Jones

There are two reasons why I have never had much interest from men:
   1. I've set my sights ridiculously high. Over the years I have tried to date Prince, Justin Timberlake, James Bond and Homer Simpson;
   2. I am neurotic, bordering on the certifiable.

Millennium Eve Eve

I think Kevin is my boyfriend because we had sex and he stayed longer than 30 minutes.

Millennium Eve

I have an oily bath, waiting for him to call.

19 March 2000

The bath is cold. He still hasn't called. I ring my best friend Jeremy to find out what to do. "Don't call him," he says. I dial Kevin's number. "Will you marry me?" I beg. "No."

20 April 2000

My three cats think I still might have a chance with Kevin. The phone rings. A man wants to interview me about my job in the media. His name is Nirpal. He is 26 years old and I think we are going to get married.

24 April 2000

He calls. "Do you want to go out to dinner?" he asks. "You're paying." "Of course," I reply.

28 April 2000

The Boyfriend looks into my eyes. "How old are you?" "31," I lie. In fact, I'm 36. "Hmm," he says, "your plastic surgery makes you look a great deal older."

15 August 2000

The Boyfriend has moved in and I am being extra nice. He is allowed to sit on my £10,000 sofa without washing obsessively first and he can cuddle me in bed, providing there is a pillow between us and he doesn't disturb the cats.

5 September 2000

The Boyfriend has moved out on my birthday. "Please come back," I plead. "I'll buy you a PlayStation, an Armani suit and let you write your novel at home while I pay for everything." "Throw in a car and I'll think about it," he says. "Done."

10 October 2002

It's our wedding day. I've spent £20,000 on hiring Babington House. I've done it. I'm married.

17 July 2003

The Husband staggers into the room. "I now weigh 17 stone," he gasps. "You've fattened me up because you hope I'll never be able to leave you. Women do still fancy me, you know." I don't think so.

23 December 2003

"You treat me like a pet," the Husband moans. This is not true. I treat him far worse. The cats get fresh tuna flakes and are allowed to sit near me.

8 April 2004

The Husband says he is feeling unfulfilled and wants a baby. "OK," I say, "let's buy one."

12 May 2004

The counsellor asks if we have considered the cultural implications of adopting an Indian child. "No," I reply thoughtfully. "I've never been to the Calcutta branch of Prada."

23 September 2004

"Not sure I want a baby any more," the Husband says. "Neither do I."

1 November 2004

The husband has been doing yoga and has lost two stone. I think he's going to leave. "Do you love me?" I ask. "Don't be so needy, and turn over to Sky Sports 1."

12 February 2005

"I've got a book deal," the Husband yells. "I'm off travelling by myself. I'll see you around." For the first time in years, I really think our marriage has a chance.

The digested read ... digested

The untreatable in pursuit of the unspeakable

The digested read ...

Middle of the road

Going East

Matthew d'Ancona

"Fancy a game of croquet?" asked Jeremy, sipping Krug.

"Ooh yes Daddy," cooed Lara, Caitlin and Ben.

"When will Mia be here?" asked Jenny.

"She said she'll be along later. She's working late with Miles."

"Hello everyone," said Mia. "Sorry I've got to leave immediately. I'm very busy."

"Never mind old thing," Ben brayed. "Now, who's going to race me to my dangerously trendy flat in the East End."

As she drove to the airport Mia reflected on the smugness of her family. Nothing bad could ever happen to them, she thought.

* * *

"Wotcha Chels."

"Hi Sylv." It had been four years since her family was tragically wiped out in the bombing. Mia was happy now as Chels, the deputy manager at the Echinacea centre in the heart of London's vibrant, multicultural East End.

"What do you think of our new assistant, Robert?"

"He's far too ugly," she said, thereby signifying she was bound to end up in bed with him later in the book.

* * *

"Hi, I'm Beatrice. I was your father's mistress for 20 years."

Mia kept quiet, reflecting on how little we sometimes know about those we love most.

* * *

"You've been dashed difficult to track down all these years," said Claude. "Come with me to the Bracknell Ball."

At the ball, Mia reflected on how far she felt from her roots, being now part of the vibrant, multicultural East End.

"I feel very guilty," Claude slurred. "Ben made his fortune laundering cash for criminals I introduced him to. That's why he was killed."

On the way home, Mia reflected on how little we often know about those we love most. She rang Rob. "I've got to have you."

* * *

"You must be Micky Hazel, the car dealer and criminal," said Mia. "What happened to my brother?"

"Girls like you get hurt asking questions like that," he menaced. "And I'm no crook."

* * *

Mia called Miles. "Now you're a top bod in the Home Office, tell me who the top gangster is."

"Try Freddy Ellis."

A bomb went off outside the Echinacea centre, killing Aasim's brother, Ali.

"It's all my fault," Mia wailed. "I shouldn't have asked about Freddy Ellis."

"Freddy Ellis has been dead for years," snapped Aasim. "The bombers were Asian."

Mia reflected on how easy it was to misread situations in London's vibrant, multicultural East End.

* * *

Mia went to visit Jean, Miles's mother. "Hello, did you know Miles's diary was stolen by Dr Muhammed's Islamist terrorists the week before your family was killed?"

Mia gave Muhammed's details to Aasim and moved to Brighton.

The digested read ... digested

The gospel according to Saint Matthew

Red Dog

Louis de Bernières

Karratha is a one-dog mining town several hundred dusty miles north of Perth. In the evenings, the men from the iron works like nothing better than to sink a few stubbies in the saloon and to reminisce about their most famous resident.

"Strewth," said Peeto. "That dog had a real talent for dropping bombs. If you were travelling any distance you had to put him in the trailer."

"Too right," replied Jack. "It was his diet, you know. He could sink a tin of Trusty in nine seconds dead."

"And the rest," added Jocko. "He could take snaggers and steaks off the barbies on the beach without anyone noticing."

"He was a real character, make no mistake," said Bruce. "He reckoned he owned the place and in a way he sort of did. Liked nothing better than to hitchhike round Western Australia. The only bloke who came close to being his owner was John."

"Yeah," chipped in Vanno. "D'you remember how he always used to have his own seat behind John on the bus."

"…and that time when Nancy tried to sit on it," Peeto continued, "Red Dog just kept nudging her off, but she wouldn't have it. After about a week they became friends, though, and Nancy was the only person he ever shared a seat with."

"Just about the only thing he did share with her," sniggered Vanno. "I heard that he interrupted John and Nancy when they were about to have a kiss, and they never had another date."

"Poor old John," sighed Jocko. It had been Jocko who had discovered John's body beside his motorbike.

"Poor old bugger," Vanno agreed, ordering another round of middies.

"Red Dog went totally bush after that," said Peeto. "He'd travel down to the beach at Freo and piss on the judges' table at the posh dog competition. And when he was shot out by Seven Mile Creek, he'd only gone and covered the wound in a field dressing by the time we got to him."

"No kidding," slurred Bluey. "I heard he'd even driven a Holden down to Adelaide and had swum over to Tazzy."

"It hasn't been the same round here since Red Dog died of strychnine poisoning," gulped Bruce, holding back the tears. "Do you think someone might write a book about him one day?"

"I guess they might."

"Will it be a bestseller?"

"Not a chance," replied Bluey before passing out.

The digested read ... digested

Captain Corelli's homage to the shaggy dog

White Mice

Nicholas Blincoe

I don't sleep at all on the night of my 20th birthday, but I still somehow wake up in bed with Jodie Kidd. The phone rings. It's my sister, Louise.

"Please come on over, Jamie," she says.

I go to her room. She's looking a mess as she's been up all night at the Versace party, but even in a mess Louise is beautiful.

"Where have you been?" she asks.

"Sleeping with Jodie Kidd," I smile.

"Duh, it was Bibi."

Well, they look the same.

"My career's going down the pan, you've got to help me," Louise insists. "The Osano show is my last chance."

I go back to Bibi. She's just OD'd on smack. I call Fred, Osano's minder. "Just like Louise," he says.

"What?"

"Don't worry," he continues, "it's got nothing to do with the rest of the story."

I pick up Fred's coat by mistake. There's something heavy in the pocket. I put my hand inside. "It's a gun."

"You've got to help me," says Osano. "My show's tonight. I really need Louise, Amanda and Bibi to make it a success."

I look at the collection. It seems stale, but I make a few alterations. The lights come on at the end of the show. Louise calls me to the front and kisses me.

"Fantastic," says Osano, "We're on all the front pages. You've got to stay with me for Milan."

Louise holes up outside Courmayeur, while I work on the designs. One evening, Louise comes into town. "You know that neither of us had a father," she says. "We came out of a clam shell."

"That's good," I reply. "Now we can sleep together."

"You realise that Louise's career is taking off again on rumours of her relationship with you," Bibi says bitchily.

"Milan was wonderful," beams Osano. "Have a ticket for Paris."

Louise joins me. "What I said about the clams," she starts, "it wasn't true."

"Ah well." We fuck all night on the sleeper.

"I'm arresting you on suspicion of murdering Osano on the train," says a cop. "Your fingerprints were on the gun."

"I can get you off," Louise remembers. "Those workers at Lyon were watching us fuck at the time in question."

"I'd rather go to prison for ever and ever than have my relationship with you made public."

The digested read ... digested

Two dim-witted siblings, utterly at home in the fashion industry, get caught up in incest and murder

Coastliners

Joanne Harris

I slipped on my *vareuse* and stepped off the ferry. I turned towards the voice. It belonged to Brismand, the hotelier from La Houssinière.

"Mado, what brings you to Le Devin?"

Why should I tell him that Maman had died in Paris? What would he care about someone who came from Les Salants, on the other side of the island.

"Bof," I replied noncommittally.

La Houssiniére had become a boom resort, but Les Salants was dying. The beach had disappeared and the houses were falling into the sea. Halfway along the *etier*, I met an enigmatic stranger.

"Who are you?" I asked.

"I am an enigmatic stranger," he replied, "but you can call me Flynn."

"How are things here?"

"Very, very *mal*."

I decided to surprise my father, Gros-Jean. He looked up and dropped the statue of Sainte-Marine into the sea.

"*Oh la la*," cried Aristide. "That has not happened since the year Guenole's cousin's son was drowned. It is bad luck."

"It is *veritablement* a crime," I lamented later with Flynn over a glass of devinnoise. "The Houssins have robbed us of our sand and our livelihoods by building a breakwater that changed the tides. Isn't there anything we could do?"

"We could build a reef in La Goulue."

"Just who are you?"

"I cannot tell you. I am *mysterieux*."

Some months later and the sands had returned to Les Salants, and with them the tourists, and the Salannais were working together to improve the village.

"It is a miracle," I whispered as Flynn sank into my arms.

"But where had the Salannais got the money to make these improvements?" I wondered out loud. Brismand smiled. It was him. He had got Flynn to make the Salannais borrow money they couldn't repay so he could take over the whole island. Flynn must be his long-lost son.

I checked the records. Gros-Jean had had an affair with Brismand's wife and Flynn was their son.

"It's not as simple as that," said Flynn. "Their son was my half-brother. I'm the result of another affair."

"So I haven't been sleeping with my brother?" The warning bell interrupted us. A tanker had run aground and the slick was heading our way.

"If I cut the reef we can reverse the tide," said Flynn. What would happen to Les Salants now? Only time would tell.

The digested read ... digested

Outsider returns to isolated French community ... *plus ça change, plus c'est la même chose*

Blue Shoes and Happiness

Alexander McCall Smith

Mma Ramotswe sat out under the hot Botswanan sun drinking a cup of red bush tea. She picked up the paper and started chuckling at the new advice column, Aunty Emang. At her age there were some things you just knew. There were the difficult problems, such as why a wheel was round, and the trivial, such as where her husband, Mr JLB Maketoni, had left his toothbrush. And it was in these very trivial problems that the only begetter of the No 1 Ladies' Detective Agency specialised.

"Men are weak," Mma Ramotswe mused. Her assistant, Mma Makutsi, sensed another profound insight was imminent. "Mr JLB Maketoni's weakness is cake."

This was indeed interesting and worthy of another cup of tea. Mma Makutsi went to the kitchen where she encountered Mr JLB Maketoni.

"Sometimes a football team wins," he said. "And sometimes it loses."

This second piece of wisdom in as many minutes was interrupted by a shout. "There's a cobra in my office," cried Mma Ramotswe.

Just then Mr Whitson, one of Mr JLB Maketoni's customers, rushed in and grabbed the snake. "You're safe now," he said. "By the way, I wonder if you can help. All the local people near the game reserve are acting strangely."

It sounded like witchcraft to Mma Ramotswe, but she decided to say nothing as a distressed young woman, wearing an apron covered in food, entered the room. "I would guess that you are a cook," said Mma Ramotswe.

"You are truly gifted with second sight," the girl answered. "I am at my wit's end. Mma Tsau is giving away free food to her husband and she thinks I am blackmailing her about it."

Mma Ramotswe drank her tea and smiled kindly. "Leave it to me."

Mma Makutsi was very disturbed. Her fiance, Phuti Radiphuti, had fallen silent when she had declared herself to be a feminist.

"You must cook him a meal to reassure him," Mma Ramotswe insisted.

Mma Makutsi followed this excellent advice to the letter, but Phuti failed to arrive. "Oh, what shall I do?" she cried.

"You must go and talk to him," said Mma Ramotswe.

"Oh, thank God, you're here," said Phuti. "I was unexpectedly called away and I was worried you might think I did not want to marry you anymore."

Mma Ramotswe sighed with the release of such unbearable tension.

A nurse darted into the office. "There's something strange about the Ugandan doctor," she said. "He's giving the wrong blood pressure pills."

Mma Ramotswe noted down the details before accompanying Mma Makutsi to buy some new shoes. "They look a little small."

Mr Polopetsi had grown concerned that Mma Ramotswe had made no attempt to solve any of her cases, so he drove to Mr Whitson's game reserve. "The locals were superstitious about the hornbill," he said later.

"Sadly, it's now a late hornbill as you put it in a box," Mma Ramotswe observed tartly. "And by the way, Aunty Emang was responsible for Mma Tsau's and the Ugandan doctor's troubles."

Mma Makutsi grinned. Mma Ramotswe had saved the day again.

"Time for tea," said Mma Ramotswe.

The digested read ... digested

Much ado about nothing

Harry Potter and the Half-Blood Prince
JK Rowling

The prime minister groaned as the minister of magic appeared. "There's trouble in the wizard world," said Cornelius Fudge. "We've got plenty of trouble in the Muggle world, too," the PM replied, happy to drop a knowing reference for the more adult readership.

Harry wasn't used to waiting until the third chapter to make an appearance. "Some years ago, I might have reacted a little petulantly," he muttered to himself, "but now I'm more grown-up I'm happy to defer my gratification."

Dumbledore appeared at the door. "I've come to take you to the Weasleys," he said kindly. "And when you return to Hogwarts, you will be having some one-to-one tuition with me. You have so much back story to catch up on that you won't be ready for your final adventure unless you do a lot of cramming."

As Harry entered Hogwarts to start his sixth year, he was aware that the usual air of excitement was missing. Everything seemed rather the same, and even the thought of playing Quidditch left him feeling a little flat.

Even his relationships with Ron and Hermione felt stale. Sure the hormones were kicking in, and there was a lot of snogging, but it all felt laboured. Couldn't everyone see that Ron was only dating Lavender to annoy Hermione and that by the end of the book Ron and Hermione were bound to be a couple?

Harry tried to remain above such goings on. He was the Chosen One after all. "For the time being," he thought, "I will express my new-found maturity by being more bad-tempered and swearing a bit." But, in time, even he couldn't resist the charms of Ginny Weasley.

A summons arrived from Dumbledore. At their previous meetings, Dumbledore had explained how Tom Riddle had become Lord Voldemort; now he wanted more. "You must persuade Professor Slughorn to share his memory with you."

"How am I going to do this?" Harry asked Hermione. "And why doesn't Dumbledore believe that Malfoy and Snape are up to no good?"

"Brilliant work," cried Dumbledore. "Now we know that Voldemort has split his soul into seven Horcruxes. We have destroyed two: only five to go before he can be defeated."

Dumbledore and Harry apparated to a cave in search of the third Horcrux, and returned to find Hogwarts under the shadow of the Dark Mark of the Death Eaters. A furious battle ensued and a central character lay dead, while Snape declared himself to be the Half-Blood Prince and disappeared with Malfoy into the night. The only message of hope was from someone who signed himself RAB.

"We have to split up, Ginny," said Harry grimly. "I can't put you in any more danger. A man's got to do what a man's got to do."

"Oh no he doesn't," Hermione and Ron chipped in. "We're coming with you."

The digested read ... digested

Back to the future

Number Ten

Sue Townsend

"How's your mum, Jack?" Edward Clare asked the policeman who stood guard outside No10.

"A little better thanks sir, but they still haven't caught the muggers."

Edward cuddled up to his wife, Adele. How lucky he was to have married the brainiest woman in Britain, and how sad that the public teased her for having such a large nose. But he supposed that was the price of being president.

"I'm just off to the Commons to save Africa," he said. On his return, he slumped in despair. He had been caught out not knowing the price of a pint of milk and had lied about taking the train.

"Do you think I'm becoming out of touch with the public?"

"We are New Labour," Alexander Macpherson, his adviser, pointed out.

"Well I think it's time I toured the country incognito to find out what the people really think." He slipped upstairs and tried on Adele's suspender belt and platinum blonde wig. "Call me Edwina."

Alexander Macpherson, Malcolm Black, the chancellor, and Ron Phillpot, the deputy PM, all sniggered. "Three little caricatures are we," they cheeped.

Jack groaned. Accompanying the PM, sorry Edwina, for a week was turning out to be a nightmare. "Everyone loves me," she would cry, as she toyed with her hair.

Edward was dangerously deluded. He patronised everyone he met. First there was Toyota on the council estate. "The government has raised benefits substantially," Edwina had said. Then there was Ali, the taxi driver. "If you've got a problem you should go to the race relations board."

Thank goodness the week was nearly up. Adele had been going bonkers in the press about the rights of amputated limbs, and Edwina was pulling the leaves off a daisy. "Bomb Iraq, don't bomb Iraq, bomb Iraq," she intoned.

Jack had problems of his own. His mum's house had been turned into a crack den.

"Crack cocaine is top of the government agenda," Edwina said.

Jack snapped: "Your policies just aren't working."

"That's not fair," Edwina sobbed. "We don't have any policies."

Edward fell into his wife's arms. "It's good to be home. God elected me president and He wants me to continue."

Malcolm Black smiled. He was going to enjoy being prime minister.

The digested read ... digested

A sledgehammer to crack a nut

Very important science and politics

The 100 Minute Bible

Michael Hilton

God created heaven and earth in six days. He then made Adam, quickly followed by Eve when he saw that Adam was bored. Their descendants proved a real disappointment, so he flooded the world and started again.

But God continued to have a lot of problems. Abraham was OK, but Jacob cheated on his brother and Joseph was such a prima donna that his brothers sold him into slavery. Moses tried to lay down the law but it took an almighty strop for anyone to notice. Joshua killed a lot of people, so did Gideon; in fact most of the judges and kings were lying psychopaths. Understandably the Jewish people needed to relax, so they sang psalms to the tune of Kumbaya.

Back in the action and it was still looking grim. A few grumpy prophets apart, it was bloodletting on a grand scale all the way. Things improved when an angel got Mary pregnant in 1BC. Joseph was very understanding about this and nine months later Jesus was born. Various shepherds and wise men paid their respects before Jesus was whisked out of town to escape Herod. He spent the next 30 years chilling out before beginning his ministry when John the Baptist was arrested. Jesus tried to avoid publicity but it was hard to keep a low profile when he was pulling off stunts like raising the dead. So it wasn't long before he collected some disciples, and from these he chose his main crew, the apostles.

Much of Jesus's teaching was captured when he spoke about the meaning of humility during the Sermon on the Mount. Apart from forgiving sins, he also said that anyone who divorces and remarries commits adultery. These views made him extremely unpopular, but calling himself the Messiah was the last straw. When he rode into Jerusalem on Palm Sunday he knew his days were numbered. On the Thursday night he was betrayed by Judas and taken before Pontius Pilate, who offered the Jews a chance to reprieve him. They refused and he was crucified and buried.

He rose from the dead on Easter Sunday. Jesus reassured his followers he was for real and over the next 40 days he made a number of other appearances before going up to heaven.

The digested read ... digested

Then I saw his face ... Now I'm a Believer

Empire: How Britain Made the Modern World

Niall Ferguson

It has long been fashionable to decry the British empire as a relic of imperial repression, and while it is not my intention to excuse its worst excesses, it is important for a good-looking historian to take a contrary position. So I contend it was also a considerable force for good.

Every iconoclast needs a neologism; mine is Anglobalisation. Other empire builders were little more than pirates, exploiting resources for their own end while seeking to impose their culture and religion on the local inhabitants. Britain, of course, was not entirely exempt in this respect but her interests lay far more in establishing a world free-trade market.

Stroll down the elegant boulevards of old Philadelphia and think of all the things that would not have existed had the world not had the benefit of my, sorry our, munificence. Sydney, Freetown, Bombay, Calcutta: all founded and built by the British. Would they have been created anyway, you might ask? Well, yes, but not nearly so well.

In 1897, the year of her Diamond Jubilee, Queen Victoria reigned supreme over 25 per cent of the world's surface; informally, through her economic activities in Latin America, her imperial reach extended still further. Wondrous times. In a spirit of unflinching altruism Britain exported its peoples and its capital to all corners of the globe, often at significant cost to itself. And where's the gratitude, that's what I want to know.

I have now reached the most solemn point of the story. It was the British Empire that alone stood up to two of the most evil empires in history in 1940 and singlehandedly saved the world from the thousand-year Reich. No greater love hath any empire than it lays down its life for its friends. In an act of Judas-like betrayal, it was the Americans, whose anti-colonial ideals sit uneasily with its own history both within and without its borders, who brought about our collapse. Britain was almost bankrupted saving the world, and America sought to expedite it in the late 1940s to acquire our markets for itself. Blame the Americans for the bloodbath of decolonisation. And what has the US given the world in return? Nothing.

All things considered, both Britain and myself can look ourselves in the mirror and be pretty damned pleased with what we see.

The digested read ... digested

Britons never, never, never shall be slaves

After the Neocons

Francis Fukuyama

The subject of this book is ostensibly US foreign policy since September 11, 2001. It's real purpose, though, is to show that my position as a neoconservative has been deeply misunderstood and that I have never been in the slightest bit inconsistent.

I have worked with some of the finest neocons – Paul Wolfowitz and Albert Wohlstetter among them – and was proud to consider myself part of their tradition. Yet even though I signed a letter urging the Clinton administration to take a more hawkish line against Iraq in 1998, I was never persuaded of the rationale for the Iraq war in 2003.

I have often asked myself whether I had in some way changed my mind in the intervening years. After much reflection I have concluded that it is neoconservatism that has changed.

The intellectual traditions of neoconservatism stretch back to the classic mid-20th century Straussian doctrine that evolved into the moral response to the relativistic and pragmatic political doctrines that formed the basis of western foreign policy against the tyranny of profoundly anti-democratic communist regimes. And sentences, such as that one, that rely on no punctuation only underline the rigour of my argument.

The early neocons were focused on democracy, human rights and the belief that US foreign policy could be used for moral purposes at times when there is scepticism about the ability of international law to solve serious security problems to the satisfaction of the US. Few could disagree with these sentiments, though I would prefer to draw a veil over events in Vietnam, Chile and Nicaragua, as these minor skirmishes fall outside my remit.

By such an assessment we are forced to recognise that Ronald Reagan was not the idiot that many people assumed. His determined hard line against the Soviet bloc in the '80s was not a piece of political opportunism waged against a regime that was already struggling with internal economic collapse; instead it was the moral catalyst that precipitated the end of communist oppression.

So how do we explain 9/11? Well, yeah but no but yeah but no but my book *The End of History* and the Last Man never said that there is a universal hunger for liberty that will inevitably lead countries to a liberal democracy and anyone that says different is a liar.

The concept of social engineering was also deeply flawed. Ethnic minorities in the US have never been grateful for anything white liberals have done for them and it should have been obvious that the Iraqis wouldn't be either.

You can see how the concept of benign hegemony became so attractive to Bush. It worked perfectly with the UK, but Donald Rumsfeld should have realised that most Jihadist terrorists are third generation westerners, and normal Iraqis have no interest in CNN.

The greatest mistake that Bush made, though, was that he did not win. And as a historian who is used to coming out on top, I find this deeply repugnant. I can no longer accept the doctrine of American exceptionalism, and we need to move to a form of international governance – something not unlike the UN and NATO – that survives on multilateral agreements. The Chad-Cameroon oil pipeline is the way forward for us all. And that really is the End of History. Until the next time.

The digested read ... digested

Je ne regrette rien

The Angry Island: Hunting the English
AA Gill

"What is it with the English?" asked the taxi driver.

"Be quiet, you impudent little man," I barked.

Later that evening, though, as I reclined on the chaise longue in my Kensington town house while the Blonde plucked my eyebrows, I reflected back on the oik's words. My publisher had made a substantial offer for my most extravagant, florid, overblown and waspish prose and all I lacked was a subject. Could this be it?

I had had the good fortune to spend the first two weeks of my life north of the border and had thus managed to avoid picking up any putrid, class-ridden affectations. So who could be better placed to expose the venereal cancer at the heart of the English?

As I wandered along Hadrian's Wall, I thought about how the Victorians had rewritten the English identity. Far from being a fair-minded people with a strong sense of history, the English are an angry race, much given to a bold assertion of a past rather than one that stands the test of argument. And I shall leave it at that.

When I received a letter asking me to pose for the National Portrait Gallery, it was impossible to demur. Yet I could not help reflecting how curious it was that I – a rebel from the wrong side of the tracks – was to become a member of the angry Establishment. But when I looked at the portentous blankness, the masterly inactivity of my picture byline, it somehow felt appropriate.

As I lazily started yet another chapter with boring reflections on myself before expanding into egregious and specious space-filling generalisations, I thought about voice. How odd that I – a Scot – should speak in the repressed anger of Received Pronunciation when even the Queen is moving towards Estuary ...

I hurried past the war memorial on Paddington station, but as I stretched out in my first-class seat, I thought about the mean-spiritedness of the English attitude to war. The English didn't die by the sword simply because they had never lived by it. Whatever that means.

The English often claim to be defined by their sense of humour, so I took it on myself to mingle with the arctophilists at a Soho comedy club. It was a depressing experience. Where was the humour in the Paki and Yid jokes to match my diatribes against the Welsh?

Stow-in-the-Wold is the worst place in the world, and I say that without exaggeration as someone who has visited Darfur. It's full of Agas and 4x4s, though I'm not sure where this is leading any more. Still, the English always say sorry in an angry fashion, so I make no apologies for wasting your time.

Like many writers running short of material, I went back to visit my school in Letchworth Garden Town, so I'd better write something about how Fascistically angry the English garden is, and while I'm on the subject of me, I should point out I used to be an alcoholic – though I was a top-up drinker, not an angry, objectionable binge drinker like the English.

The English like queues, losing at sport and nostalgia. All classic Jungian signs of anger. Indeed, left to themselves, the English are destined to be remembered as little more than a cul-de-sac in history. Much like this book.

The digested read ... digested

AA puts the English on the couch but merely exposes himself

A Briefer History of Time

Stephen Hawking

The title of this book differs by only two letters from *A Brief History of Time* that I wrote in 1988. That book stayed on the bestseller list for 237 weeks; a remarkable feat for a book that no one understood. Three years ago, I attempted to simplify my ideas in *The Universe in a Nutshell*, but I now gather that no one understood that, either. So, I'm now giving you a third and final chance. At the very least, you will begin to grasp the concept of circular time.

So pay attention. As Einstein points out, time may be relative, but mine's more valuable than yours. We're searching for a grand unified theory, but haven't got one, because general relativity and quantum mechanics are inconsistent with one another. So let's start with Newton, who gave us the three laws of motion, which describe how bodies react to forces, and the theory of gravity.

Newton refused to accept the lack of absolute space, even though his laws implied it, but he believed wholeheartedly in absolute time. This was a mistake, as everyone has their own four-dimensional spacetime. Einstein's theory of general relativity is based on the revolutionary suggestion that gravity is not a force like other forces, but a consequence of the the fact that spacetime is curved. Light rays, too, must follow geodesics in spacetime, as relativity predicts light will be bent by gravitational fields.

Thanks to the Doppler effect, we know that the universe is expanding as the light-shifts of stars veer towards the red end of the spectrum. If you listen carefully, you can also pick up cosmic noise, which is, in fact, the glow of microwave radiation from the early formation of the universe. So how did the universe start?

All solutions to Einstein's equations point to the fact that at some time in the past the universe was squashed into a single point with zero size. At this point, which we call big bang, the density of the universe and the curvature of spacetime would have been infinite, so unfortunately all theories of cosmology break down.

Still, with me? Probably not. But never mind. I shall carry on regardless. One second after big bang, the universe would have contained mostly photons, electrons and neutrinos, and their anti-particles, together with some protons and neutrons. Colliding photons might produce an electron and a positron, if they met up they would annihilate each other, but the reverse process is not so easy. Eventually, when the temperature had fallen to allow the strong force to take effect we'd begin to see the nuclei of deuterium. From then on it was downhill through supernovae and black holes to the present day.

But how do we resolve the problem of singularity? Through supersymmetry? String theory? 10-dimensional space? These are only partial explanations. All we can say for certain is that it is possible to write five sentences that make sense on their own, but when put together in a paragraph are intelligible only to God. And me.

The digested read ... digested

Third Time Unlucky

Everything Bad Is Good for You: How Popular Culture is Making Us Smarter

Steven Johnson

This book is an old-fashioned work of persuasion that aims to convince you of one thing: that I am one of the most influential social commentators of the 21st century. To this end I have decided to take the generally accepted premise that modern culture is dumbing down and argue the opposite, as this will guarantee me a lot of attention.

No one will take me seriously unless this work has a veneer of intellectual rigour, so allow me to introduce you to the Sleeper Curve. This is the pretentious name I have given to the premise that the popular media – usually dismissed as lowbrow fluff – is actually making our minds much sharper.

Take video games. The common view is that the people who play them are witless, atavistic sociopaths. Nothing could be further from the truth. Modern games have a free-form structure that constantly challenges the player to interact with the environment and make complex decisions.

By contrast, books deliver a linear narrative that rarely forces the reader to think. What book can teach you how to cut someone up with a chainsaw, hide their body in a dumpster and evade capture by crawling through a ventilation duct?

With this in mind, you might ask why I am choosing to publish this work in book form. The answer is simple. The Sleeper Curve shows that gamers are too clever to be taken in by this nonsense.

You can make a similar claim for television. Is *Hill Street Blues* better than *Starsky & Hutch*? Series such as *The West Wing* carry several different plot lines in a single episode: this would have baffled viewers in the 1960s. Now your average teenager can keep track of *Hollyoaks* and *Crossroads* while doing their homework.

Reality TV shows are the supreme example of dumbing up, as they make huge demands on a viewer's emotional intelligence. It's up to you, and you alone, to understand the social nuances of *Celebrity Love Island* and to work out if there's anything at all going on in Abi Titmuss's head, because she really doesn't have a clue herself.

Not many people claim that the internet has been a force of cultural deprivation, but I need you to assume everyone does say that or my already slender book will come to a premature conclusion. It's just not true that the internet is a passive medium that makes few learning requirements of its users. U can snd msgs and make lots of new friends. Visit stevenberlinjohnson.com to see how hunky I am.

Films are also more complex. The first *Star Wars* picture had far fewer characters than the first part of *Lord of the Rings*. The Sleeper Curve says that our modern trash is better than our parents' trash. And as the philosospher James Flynn has proved, we are all now much brighter thanks to this trash. Last century's brainiac is today's simpleton.

The digested read ... digested

Nothing this bad is good for you

Freakonomics: A Rogue Economist Explores the Hidden Side of Everything

Steven D Levitt & Stephen J Dubner

The most brilliant economist in the world brakes to a halt and wonders why the tramps buy $50 headphones.

In the summer of 2003 the *New York Times* sent the journalist Stephen J Dubner to interview the heralded maverick economist Steven D Levitt. What were the chances of two men with extraneous initials being attracted to one another? Higher than you might think. Levitt recognised in Dubner a man with a gift for hagiography, while Dubner knew a meal ticket when he saw it.

Anyone living in the US in 1990 could have been forgiven for being scared out of his skin. Crime was expected to rocket out of control within a decade. What happened? It went down. Why? More police? No. It was because the abortion laws changed. All those who would have grown up to be criminals were never born.

Ever wondered why an estate agent sells her house for more than you? She's better at her job? No. The extra $10,000 you might get is only worth about $150 to her. But when she sells her own house the full $10,000 extra is hers. See. It's simple when you think about it.

Levitt is considered a demi-god, one of the most creative people in economics and maybe in all social science.

If morality is the way we would like the world to work, then economics is how it actually does work. Freakonomics works on a number of premises. 1) Incentives are the cornerstone of modern life. 2) Conventional wisdom is often wrong. 3) Experts use their informational advantage to serve their own agenda. 4) Readers' gullibility should never be underestimated.

Levitt is a noetic butterfly that no one has pinned down, but is claimed by all.

What do schoolteachers and sumo wrestlers have in common? They all cheat. I know this will come as a terrible shock but dreary data proves it is true.

Levitt is one of the most caring men in the universe.

Why do so many drug dealers live with their mom? Amazingly, I can prove that most of them earn far less than you might imagine.

Levitt is genial, low-key and unflappable.

What makes a perfect parent? Research has shown that making a child watch TV in a library is the most effective way of ensuring he gets top grades.

Levitt is about to revolutionise our understanding of black culture. Even for Levitt this is new turf.

Black parents often give their children different names. A boy called Deshawn is less likely to get a job interview than someone called Steven. Maybe Deshawn should change his name.

The digested read ... digested

What is the probability that a collection of often trivial and obvious data will be passed off as brilliance? Regrettably high

Mind the Gap: Class in Britain Now

Ferdinand Mount

"Class divisions are fading in Britain." We have heard it said so often, it must be true. I have even said as much myself. But looking through my notes once more, something made me hesitate. It wasn't, perhaps, the very obvious inequalities in Britain; it was the cultural impoverishment of the lower orders. They are not just worse off in relation to the very rich; they lack even the lowly and trivial ambitions of their parents.

You might wonder why someone like me should care. Well, I don't really, but I've got a lot of time on my hands and I don't need the cash, so I thought I'd turn my brilliant mind to the subject. You see, it's no fun patronising the working class when they behave like a lumpen mass of shell-suited morons.

It's true that more people have washing machines and telephones than they did 30 years ago (*The Times*, 2003). But that is not proof of a narrowing of the class divide. In real terms, there is a greater disparity of earnings between the very rich and the very poor. People's names also give a great deal away. How many proles do you know called Ferdinand?

We are also further than ever from equality of opportunity. Can you imagine the reaction of a worthwhile publisher to the idea of a book on class written by a common person? In fact, it is intellectually impossible for a common person to have conceived such a notion (Lord Snooty, *Beano*, 1964).

David Lodge has described *The Time Machine* as "one of the most desolating myths in modern literature" (*Language of Fiction*, 1966). Yet HG Wells's tale has a resonance today; for the Elois and the

Morlocks read the Uppers and the Lowers. The strata are rigidly defined. Moreover, governments of both hues have reinforced the divisions through their social policy.

The Lowers have had everything they held dear ripped from them. Their dependence on the church has been undermined, along with their noble aspirations to wedlock and the nuclear family (Charles Moore, *Daily Telegraph*, 1995-2003); they have been nannied into filthy estates where they all smoke crack, joyride cars and have their senses dulled by cable TV. If one person is responsible for this it is Rupert Murdoch; at least that's what I would have written were I not a columnist for the *Sunday Times*. So I blame the BBC instead. The director general has forgotten the meaning of the words "*Dei omnipotenti templum hoc artium...*" engraved in the hall of Broadcasting House.

What is to be done, you may ask? We Uppers must do our best to make the Lowers feel more wanted by visiting them in prison. And those who are out on bail should be given a plot of land to build their own hovels. I shall stay in Islington.

The digested read ... digested

The political manifesto for the Monster Raving Loony party

Hooking Up

Tom Wolfe

The morning one of the Valley's new firms sprang its IPO, the company's 40-year-old CEO instantly became worth $9m. Four and a half hours later, he took his Ferrari for a spin and did just that. The car went through a guardrail and he was killed. The Valley took it as the dark side of the Force, but others saw it otherwise. That there was still a God.

Internet gurus tell us that the computer is a brain and that if we get a sufficient number of them, billions, operating all over the world in a single seamless Web, we will converge on a superbrain that overarches petty nationalism and racial competition. But let me assure you that all the internet does is speed up information and partially eliminate chores. All else is Digibabble. If you don't believe me, tell me why SAT scores are falling?

The answer may be found among the new neuroscientists. We are what we are. Our brains are hot-wired, a genetically predetermined series of electromagnetic switches. There is no such thing as consciousness, guilt or freewill. This is not a popular line of enquiry, and even as I write the evolutionary apologists are fighting a revisionist battle for our souls. I predict that as all the accepted 21st-century mantras slip back into the primordial ooze, a new theory will emerge. It will feel solid. And it will be named God.

Which brings me nicely to me. I feel a little uncomfortable including my magnificent 1965 pastiche of the *New Yorker*, because today it might not seem quite so remarkable as it was then. But let me assure you that its brilliance has stood the test of time and that I have emerged as the only writer with the genius to give

America the literature it deserves. Take my last novel, *A Man in Full*. Eleven years in the writing, I grant you, but the public and the critics adored it. I mention this only because others have mentioned it, not out of self-regard.

And who should be the only dissenters? Norman Mailer, John Irving and John Updike, the three writers who have done the most in recent years to traduce us with their bumbling musings. There will, and there must be a saviour from their myopia.

God bless America and God bless me. Me, me, me, God, me, me, God, me.

The digested read ... digested

America's most stylish essayist passes judgment on God, Mammon and the land of the brave

The digested read

Try-hards

The Sea House

Esther Freud

Max Meyer was in Steerborough to see if he might do a painting of houses. How closely the town resembled Southwold, he might have thought had he been less self-obsessed. Was it really eight years since the end of the war? The pain never left him.

* * *

Lily looked round the cottage she had rented for the summer. Steerborough was the ideal spot for her research; she would never want for an organic loaf. She started on the first Lehmann letter, dated 1931. "My dear Elsa, I am here in Frankfurt because I am a very important architect. You are so lucky that I love you. Tell me you adore me. Klaus." Should she phone Nick? Would he ever say he loved her? It was so hard being such a victim.

* * *

Gertrude interrupted Max's solipsism. "I've invited the Lehmanns over to dinner." Max nodded. They should be able to share his pain as they too had suffered as Jews in Nazi Germany. Why could he not include the Lehmanns' house in his painting?

* * *

"I've got to go," said Nick. "There's work to do if we want to win the contract. Work for me. I need someone to sharpen my pencil." Lily sobbed. He had driven the 100 miles to Steerborough merely for a fuck. How she longed to be an architect like him, and yet how she longed to be different. She went for a walk on the beach. A salt-of-the-earth artisan walked by. Maybe she could be happy.

* * *

"Oh Elsa, my ears are hurting so much," Max cried. "Only you who have also suffered can understand." Elsa paused. "Klaus is away. Come with me to the Sea House and fill me with love."

* * *

Lily smiled at Grae, the strong, silent wife-beater and suddenly realised he wasn't a wife-beater after all. Though not artistic, he was still sensitive and soulful. "Come into my tent," he growled. "Fill me with love," she whispered.

* * *

Gertrude stared at Max's painting. A week ago it had been lifeless; now it teemed with humanity And there was the Lehmanns' house.

At the Sea House Elsa took Max in her arms. "I am with child."

* * *

Lily lay in Grae's arms. "Am I with child?" she wondered. It was strange how little guilt she felt about Nick. Maybe she wouldn't always be a victim, after all. "Oh look, you've got your period," said Grae.

* * *

The sea walls broke and the waters rose in the Sea House. Max and Elsa held each other tight as they heard the rescuers approach. "Dear Max, Klaus died rescuing you, but Elsa has had twins, Sincerely, Gertrude."

* * *

"I'm going back to my wife," grunted Grae. Lily tried not to cry. She rang Nick. "I've always loved you," he said.

The digested read ... digested

Victims of a parallel world unite in Southwold

The Fit

Philip Hensher

When I woke up, my wife had gone. Where my wife's head should have been on the pillow was a letter. I read it. Then I started to hiccup.

"!" I gulped.

I went out into the garden. A strange girl wandered into the garden.

"Who are you?" she asked.

"!" I hiccupped. "I'm John." My wife's name is Janet. I know what you're thinking. Janet and John. "And – ! – who are you?"

"I'm Susie," she said. "I'm just one of those strange characters that turn up from time to time in pretentious books for no apparent reasons. You won't see me again until the end."

I went indoors to get dressed. It wasn't hard as all my clothes are the same. Janet used to find that strange. I'm an indexer by profession, but a lot of people don't find it very interesting. I like to think I'm an idiot savant; really I'm just an idiot.

Janet and I live in a very expensive house in Putney. She was given it by her ex-lover, Gareth. My family are rather envious, especially my sister Sarah, who was about to get married.

"I'm Wasia," said the attractive Indian woman standing next to me at the reception.

"!" I replied. I didn't know her. She was a conceptual artist gatecrashing the wedding. I turned to Sarah. "Isn't it sad Franky isn't here?"

"You spoil everything."

It's Brenda, here. John's mother. I'd like to tell you how my eldest daughter was murdered. It doesn't add anything to the story, but it takes up lots of pages and gives an impression of pathos.

My phone rang. It was Janet. "I'm in India," she said. She was lying. Her note had said the reason she'd left me was because of my wardrobe. I searched it and found a phone number. It was bound to be Gareth's. She was back with him.

"Let me meet your family," said Wasia, after we'd been to a nightclub and I'd written an unconvincing chapter on cocaine and ecstasy.

"!" I replied, and she picked up her camera.

Later that week I appeared on *Remember This*, a radio programme about lost love. I told everyone Janet had gone back with Gareth. Gareth phoned in to say he was happily married, and that the number wasn't his. It turned out to be the local cinema.

"I hate you," said Wasia. "You take no interest in me." But she still invited me to her show of photographs of my family. People laughed.

* * *

Janet here. I didn't go to India. I stayed in Greece. I only married John because I had contempt for him and his clothes. Now I've told him I'm in Australia, and anywhere I go now can only bring me closer to him.

Susie turned up and tidied the house and then Janet reappeared. "!" I said. "You're back." My hiccups vanished as she traced a four-letter word. But I only picked up the first L.

The digested read ... digested

It's a hiccup for John, but a migraine for everyone else

Beyond Black

Hilary Mantel

Colette put her head round the dressing-room door. "Ready?" she asked. Alison slid her size-20 frame out of her seat, stepped over Morris, who was playing with himself on the floor, and walked out on stage.

"Anyone out here called Sarah-Anne?" she called out. "Your granny wants you to know she's fine."

* * *

It was when Gavin left that Colette became interested in the paranormal. She tried tarot and palm-readers, but it was not until she met Big Al that she found her purpose in life. "You need a manager," she said, and Big Al gently acquiesced.

Alison had known she had a talent for speaking to the other side since she was a child. She gave the audience a rosy vision of the afterlife, in which relatives met up and tumours were reversed. But she knew only a nasty chaos lay ahead.

"Come on, you fat cow," sneered Morris, "do your worst." In life Morris had been one of the many men, along with Capstick and Aitkenside, her mother had let abuse her. In death, he was her spirit guide, the man who taunted her with tales of "Old Nick".

* * *

At the start of their business relationship, around the time of Princess Diana's death, Colette and Al had been inseparable. By day they drove to events and by night they returned to the house Al had bought for them. "I suppose it doesn't matter if the neighbours think we're lezzies," Colette had reasoned.

But after a few years, everything became stale. For the best part of 300 pages there had been predictable, repetitive episodes with Morris and his mates, droll psychic encounters with the general public, and dry *aperçus* about suburban life, and Colette reluctantly concluded the book was going nowhere. "Surely Big Al could have predicted just how dull this would be," she thought.

* * *

But even Big Al was forced to admit some resolution was required. So when a vagrant moved into their garden shed, she decided to make him her good work. Colette called her a stupid overweight sucker for being taken in by Mart's hard luck story, but Big Al was determined to help him, so she took to sharing takeaways with him.

"If I'm nice to Mart, maybe Morris will leave me alone," she thought, as memories of her childhood flooded back. Who had her father been?

"That tramp has hung himself," shouted Colette. "It's all your fault, you stupid bitch. I'm going back to Gavin."

In the spirit world, Morris was regretting having killed Mart. "I didn't realise he was her good work," he muttered. "She's cast me adrift. Perhaps Old Nick was her father."

Big Al snoozed contentedly in the back of the car as her new friend Maureen drove her along the M25.

The digested read ... digested

It ain't over till the fat lady snores

Judge Savage

Tim Parks

Do you ever get the feeling you've been set up? Here I am, one of the youngest-ever black judges, and I'm called Daniel Savage. This is Parksie's idea of a joke – he wants to challenge all your assumptions. Actually, I wasn't originally called Savage, mutter mutter, I was adopted by an upper-class white family and was given their name.

Hilary's just about stopped giving me a hard time over the affair I had with Jane. I had to move out for a while but now we're buying a new house, I'm getting her a piano, and we're selling our old flat to our friends Martin and Christine. Mutter mutter. Martin's my oldest lawyer friend, but he's gone a bit odd.

Who was that on the phone? shrieks Hilary. As if I could tell her about Minnie, the Korean juror I shagged a couple of times. Someone at work, I reply. She doesn't believe me. Neither do my children. Tom just plays with his computer and Sarah has deliberately failed her A-levels.

This is hard work, isn't it? I can tell you don't really like me, but it's not easy having a personality when you're made of cardboard and only really exist as the emblematic anti-hero. I could kill Parksie, I could.

Minnie left another message, she says she's in trouble, mutter mutter. I go round to see her family and that's the last I remember. You've been in a coma, says Hilary when I come round in hospital. Who did that to you? the police ask. No idea, I lie.

I must find Minnie to find out if she's all right. Sure, I know where she is, offers my brother Frank – the old colonel's real son and the genuine black sheep. Nice irony that, Parksie. I'm all right except I'm pregnant, says Minnie. Ah well, mutter mutter, I'd better go.

Christine tries to kiss me when I go round to see Martin. You should tell the truth, he says before I go back to try one of those tricky race cases black judges always end up with in second-rate fiction.

I make a statement to the police and tell Hilary all about Minnie and the Koreans. I can feel my life falling apart. Hilary gets hysterical, mutter mutter, and I get kicked out.

I'm going through the motions here. Martin dies and it turns out he was a paedophile. What was all that about, mutter mutter?

I start hanging around with prostitutes. I think everyone hates me now. Not that there's much to hate. The police phone. The Koreans have been arrested on an immigration scam. Minnie calls asking for help. I invite her to my hotel. She dies in my bed. How inconsiderate is that? Mutter mutter.

Judge Savage pours out a powerful measure of a sleeping drug and swallows it gratefully. Several hundred pages too late.

The digested read ... digested

Daniel Savage's cartoon life unravels around him spectacularly quickly. But still far too slowly for everyone else

The digested read ...

The Brooklyn Follies

Paul Auster

I was looking for a quiet place to die. Someone recommended Brooklyn, so I rented an apartment there. The oncologist had said my lung cancer was in remission but I didn't necessarily believe him; so when my daughter, Rachel, came down to cheer me up I told her I didn't really give a damn about her or her platitudes. You could say that I've never been good at relationships.

Enough about me. This book is really about my nephew, Tom. To say I was amazed when I found him working in Harry Lightman's secondhand bookshop would be an understatement. When I'd last seen him, he'd been a bright, good-looking man. Now, he was overweight and beaten. I took him out for lunch.

Tom told me about how his life had gone downhill since college, how he had become estranged from his sister, Aurora, who'd got mixed up in porn and drugs, how he fancied this woman whom he called Beautiful Perfect Mother (BPM) and how he'd come to work for Harry.

"He's not who he seems," he confided. "He's been in prison for an art scam."

None of this bothered me and I soon made friends with both BPM and Harry, but everything changed when Aurora's 10-year-old daughter, Lucy, turned up unexpectedly at the bookshop.

Lucy refused to speak so I was unable to discover her mother's whereabouts. In desperation, I arranged for her to stay with some relations in Vermont and headed up-country.

Unknown to us, Lucy tipped several tins of Coke in the gas tank and we came to a halt for five days at The Chowder Inn.

Such are the whims of fate. Here in the cocoon of the unreal, Tom met Honey and I decided Lucy should live with me after all. And here, we heard that Harry had died after he had been threatened with exposure over a forged Hawthorne manuscript.

On our return to Brooklyn the sense of fluffy planets colliding in a rollercoaster of mixed metaphors and over-blown set pieces hurtling towards a series of neatly-contrived happy endings continued apace. Harry had left the building and the business to Tom, who settled down and lived happily ever after with Honey. *Ah!* Lucy started talking and moved in with Tom and Honey. *Ah!* Rachel and I were reconciled and she soon announced I would be a grandfather. *Ah!*

I tracked down Aurora to a strange religious sect in North Carolina where she was being held prisoner by her wicked second husband, David. *Boo!*

"Thank you so much for saving me, Uncle Nathan," she cried. "Even though I wasn't really in any danger and could have walked out any time, I am grateful to you for rescuing me." *Ah!*

Aurora came back with me to Brooklyn and started a committed lesbian relationship with BPM who had left her beastly husband. *Risqué but Ah!*

And me? I had started a relationship with BPM's mother. *Ah!* As I kissed her one night, I felt a crushing pain in my left arm. *Boo!* Was I going to die? No. *Ah!*

But I am an important novelist, so I can't let things end like this. As I left the hospital it was 8am on September 11, 2001.

The digested read ... digested

A Fairytale of New York

The Good Life

Jay McInerny

Corinne kicked her Manolo heels around their TriBeCa loft, dropping names as easily as she mixed her metaphors. "Thank God, Salman and Bret aren't coming to dinner after all," she simpered, drinking Cristal as she kissed the twins goodnight.

"It's a disaster," screeched Russell. "I've run out of thyme."

Corinne's phone rang as the last guests staggered home. "Jim and Cody want to discuss my screenplay," she yelled, putting on her Dolce & Gabbana coat.

"I need strange pussy," said Cody. "Fuck me and the waitress."

Corinne felt strangely flattered, but demurred.

***

"Isn't this dress just beyond?" said Sasha.

Luke gazed at her as she stretched out like an odalisque. Since making his fortune and quitting his job, he had lost direction. "Do we have to go to the ball?"

"Of course. It's to die for. And I've invited Ashley, too."

He watched Sasha press herself against Melman, while Ashley drank cocktails. He was losing his wife and daughter.

***

Luke emerged from the wreckage. He felt so guilty that he had survived. If only he hadn't overslept he would have been killed in the attack. Through the dust, he spied a grey angel.

"I'm Corinne," she said. "My friend Jim died here yesterday and I need to help."

"I'm Luke," he replied. "My friend Guillermo also died. Perhaps we should serve in the soup kitchen to heal the traumas of our lives."

Corinne bathed in the warm glow of her own portentousness. From now on there would not be a single feeling – however banal – that she would not indulge over several dozen pages at a time.

Russell felt overwhelmed by remorse. The events of September 11 made him want to tell Corinne he had had an affair. Corinne read his email. Was this the excuse she needed to have an affair with Luke? Only a great deal of introspective angst would tell.

"We need to buy a third house," Sasha squeaked. Luke longed for Corinne's depth and wisdom. Was it possible she might feel attracted to him?

"Ashley has overdosed and is in rehab," Luke wailed. "I feel so guilty I was never there for her as a child."

Corinne felt a surge of solipsistic empathy. "I feel so guilty I made my sister provide the eggs for the twins."

Luke felt an electric shock of relief. "I feel so guilty that I never talked to my mother again after she had an affair."

Their collective guilt exploded into a frenzy of love and the Nantucket waves crashed to the shore as he entered her.

"You're my first, my last, my everything," Corinne and Luke gulped in unison. "But I feel so guilty."

Russell forced his cock inside Corinne's ass. Now she knew she need never feel guilty again.

"I've made up with Ashley and my mum," Luke whispered. "Now we can be together."

* * *

Luke and Sasha bumped into Russell and Corinne at the Nutcracker. Somehow Luke just knew it was over.

The digested read ... digested

Four New Yorkers in a failed search for a personality

In the Hands of the Taliban

Yvonne Ridley

September 11 wasn't like a normal Tuesday; instead of taking my usual long lunch at the Ivy, I happened to be going through my expenses at my desk so I actually watched the second plane hit the WTC live on TV. My first thoughts were "Wow, the world's never going to be the same again," swiftly followed by "This is a fantastic story, I must fly to New York immediately." Sadly this wasn't possible, so I nipped across the road to Stammy's to sink a few pints of Lynne's infamous Pimm's.

I flew to Islamabad on the Friday as things were hotting up in Pakistan and the news desk felt my vast experience of the Middle East would be invaluable.

Islamabad turned out to be a real nightmare. You couldn't get a drink, the food was crap and even the cigarettes were second rate. As I lay in my hotel room, I did vaguely wonder whether I should have told my eight-year-old daughter, Daisy, where I was, but then I remembered that we had such a trusting relationship there was no need.

I filed a couple of stories and texted my new boyfriend asking whether he had read them. He replied that he hadn't. He's now very much an ex!

I needed a scoop. Eventually I found two guides who would take me into Afghanistan. I couldn't see much through my burka as the truck crossed the valley, but I sensed that the Afghans were a proud and independent people and that the countryside was nice.

Just as we were about to cross back into Pakistan, disaster struck when my guides were stopped by a Talib. I rushed forward to be arrested too. I was thrown into a jail in Jalalabad, where the toilets were exceptionally unpleasant. On the whole, even though I was very stroppy, my captors treated me with respect, and I even managed to keep a prison diary on the inside of my toothpaste carton. Booze, nil; calories, nil; cigs, not enough. How hard was that!

Several days later, I was moved to Kabul where I was able to keep up the spirits of those poor aid workers who were also being held captive. When the first bombs went off, I assured them we were in no danger as the US could pinpoint their targets to the nearest tree.

To my surprise, I was released the following day. It was so nice to come home and have a drink, and I was very moved to read all my emails telling me what a wonderful and important person I am. I must say that I thoroughly agree.

The digested read ... digested

Narcissistic journalist dresses up as John Simpson, gets caught, causes a great deal of aggravation, gets let out and tries to cash in

Avenger

Frederick Forsyth

Freddy put down his copy of the *Daily Telegraph* and sighed. The stock market hadn't been kind to the Master Storyteller. He pressed the secret panel of his large oak desk. It was time to bring his trusty Montblanc fountain pen out of retirement.

* * *

Anyone watching the 51-year-old wheeze along the New Jersey streets could have been forgiven for not realising they were in the presence of the fittest, cleverest, noblest and most dangerous man in the world.

Calvin Dexter had been brought up the hard way. He fought in Vietnam and he and his senior officer became the most feared Tunnel Rats in the US army. Their nicknames were Mole and Badger.

When the war ended Cal put himself through law school and became a brilliant public defender. After his wife and child tragically died he left the law to disappear into anonymity. Only those who really needed his services would know where to find him.

* * *

It had been many years since Ricky Colenso had disappeared in the former Yugoslavia. At last, his grandfather, the Canadian billionaire Steve Edmond, had a lead. A body had been discovered in a slurry pit and the suspect was Serbian warlord Zoran Zilic.

"I don't care how much it costs, I want him brought to justice," said Edmond.

It was June 2001.

* * *

Cal checked the small ads. He had a job. His superb tracking skills quickly picked up the trail. His aircraft had been spotted in al-Fujairah, and from that it was relatively simple to deduce that Zilic was now in a heavily protected fortress in Surinam.

It was July 2001.

* * *

CIA chief Paul Deveraux leant forward and spoke to his deputy, Kevin McBride. "We can't let anything happen to Zilic," he said. "We know al-Qaida is about to launch a major attack on the west and Zilic has promised to lead us to Osama bin Laden."

It was August 2001.

* * *

"So," thought Cal, "the Americans are on to me. Shouldn't make much difference."

Armed only with a penknife, Cal skipped through the inhospitable terrain, waltzed past the private militia, swam through the piranha-infested stream, pirouetted through the dogs and the minefields and boarded Zilic's private jet.

"You are coming with me to face justice in the land of the brave and the home of the free," he snarled.

It was September 9, 2001.

* * *

"Project Peregrine is dead in the water," said Deveraux. "Ten more days and Bin Laden would have been ours. But just who did tip off Avenger?"

McBride smiled to himself, the outline of a badger tattoo just visible through his shirt.

It was September 10, 2001.

The digested read ... digested

This year's winner of the Jeffrey Archer prize for creative writing

False Impression

Jeffrey Archer

9/10 – Lady Victoria Wentworth never heard the young woman break into her stately home. Minutes later she lay dead with her throat slit and her ear removed.

9/11 – Today Fenston would get his hands on the Van Gogh. Few suspected that behind his facade as a respected banker lay one of Ceauşescu's most loyal cronies who had amassed a fabulous horde of impressionist art by getting rich collectors to borrow money at ridiculous rates of interest and then killing them.

Anna Petrescu, the world's most fragrant expert on impressionist paintings, entered the North Tower and took the elevator for her meeting with her boss.

"The Wentworth Van Gogh should be sold to Nakamura," she said. "That way, she can pay her debts and keep her home."

"You're fired," Fenston yelled and left. Anna went to her office and the walls exploded around her. She was the last person to leave the tower alive.

"Hmm," she thought. "Everyone will assume I'm dead. Maybe I can use that to my advantage and save the Wentworth Van Gogh."

9/12 – Anna ran the last six miles to the Canadian border and flew to London.

"Aha," said Fenston. "She's gone to London via Canada." He picked up the phone and called Krantz, his personal 4ft 11in female Romanian assassin.

Jack observed Anna and Fenston from afar. "Maybe if I repeat the fact that Anna has gone to London via Canada it will make it seem less ridiculous," he told his CIA minder.

9/13 – Anna arrived in London, hijacked the Van Gogh, had a secret meeting with Victoria's sister, Lady Arabella, and left for Bucharest with a parcel.

"She's leaving for Bucharest," said Krantz, getting on the same plane.

"She's leaving for Bucharest," said Jack, getting on the same plane.

9/14 – Anna met with her old art teacher and asked him a special favour. "Because of all the charitable works you have done, I cannot refuse," he said.

"She's leaving for Tokyo," said Krantz, getting on the same plane.

"She's leaving for Tokyo," said Jack, getting on the same plane.

9/15 – "You are a remarkable woman, Miss Petrescu," bowed Nakamura. "I will do as you say".

Krantz hung on to the bumper of Nakamura's car for 40 miles before holding up the driver. She ripped open the parcel. It was the wrong painting.

"She's going back to Bucharest," said Krantz, getting on the same plane.

"She's going back to Bucharest," said Jack, getting on the same plane.

9/16 – Anna had another secret meeting with her art teacher before leaving for London. The taxi driver shot Krantz in the shoulder. "That's for all those who died under Ceausescu," he muttered.

9/18 – Fenston unwrapped the Van Gogh. "It's a fake," sneered the insurers.

9/19 – Jack phoned his minder. "Krantz escaped from 17 guards at the hospital."

9/20 – Arabella, Anna and Nakamura celebrated the sale of the Van Gogh.

"Not so fast," laughed Krantz. Arabella, who had a touch of Margaret Thatcher's steel, blasted her with a shotgun.

Jack rushed in. "I've just realised that Fenston is wearing one of Victoria's earrings, so everything's sorted." He gazed into Anna's millpond eyes. "Come back to Grantchester with me."

The digested read ... digested

Crook tries to make money out of 9/11. Just like his characters

Shock
and awe

Digital Fortress

Dan Brown

Tankado died with the three good fingers of his shrivelled hand pointing heavenward.

Susan Fletcher was woken by the phone. It was David. "I've got to postpone," he said. "Something's come up." The phone rang again. It was Strathmore, deputy head of the NSA. "Something's come up," he said. "Come in."

Few people have heard of the NSA. Fewer still have heard of TRANSLTR, the world's most powerful computer, buried deep underground in NSA headquarters. It can decipher any code.

"It's bad, Susan," he said. "Our ex-employee Tankado has created an algorithmal code TRANSLTR can't decipher. He has a partner called NDAKOTA who has the pass code. That's where you come in. I need you to trace his untraceable email address."

David was having a bad day. He hadn't told Susan that Strathmore had sent him to Spain to get the code from Tankado's ring. Now Tankado was dead, the businessman and the prostitute who had taken the ring were dead, the American punk who had bought the ring off the prostitute was dead, and the assassin was after him. Worse still, the ring was a red herring: there was no code.

Greg Hales entered the NSA inner sanctum. Susan thought he might be NDAKOTA. "It's not right we should be able to spy on ordinary Americans," he said.

"TRANSLTR has already saved America from two terrorist attacks," she replied.

"Then how come we couldn't stop 9/11?"

"Because this book was published in the US in 1998 and it's only getting an outing in the UK to cash in on *The Da Vinci Code.*"

Susan's superfast decryption programme suggested Tankado and NDAKOTA had the same email. Of course, she thought, they're anagrams of one another. She looked up to see Greg Hales kill a security officer.

Strathmore was starting to panic. He would have to tell Susan. "It's not an algorithmal code," he said. "It's a worm. I was trying to add a mutation that would allow us to read every secret in the world. But I've failed and now all America's secrets are going to be available online unless we get this code."

Susan and Strathmore cornered Hales. "It's Strathmore," yelled Hales. "He killed the security officer." But no one believed him and he died a nasty death.

Strathmore loved Susan. He had no regrets about telling the assassin to kill David.

Susan read Strathmore's pager. David was dead and Strathmore was bad. He died a horrible death, too. She called the NSA head. "We've got two minutes to save the world," she said. "The code must be a prime number."

She stared at images of Tankado's three fingers.

"Saved with only seconds to spare," said the NSA head.

The phone rang. It was David. "I'm alive. Marry me."

The digested read ... digested

Top US intelligence boffin solves a seven-letter anagram and helps save the world

The Enemy

Lee Child

It was New Year's Day 1990. The Berlin Wall was half down. The phone rang. "Reacher here," I said.

"General Kramer's dead. Heart attack."

The short sentences got my pulse racing. "I'm on it."

What was a general doing with a $20 whore? Why was he so far out of town?

I checked the crime scene. Briefcase missing.

The phone rang. "Mrs Kramer's been found dead. Head stoved in. Crowbar."

Coincidence? Hardly. I picked out a rookie MP. "Your name?"

"Summer," she replied.

"You're the love interest."

"So where's the agenda for your meeting with Kramer?" I asked Coomer and Vasell.

"No idea," they lied. I hated generals. I hated this job. Why was I here? I could tell it would turn out badly.

The phone rang. "Mum's dying," said my brother. I flew to France.

"Hi Reacher," my mother gasped. "I'm dying."

"You've been awol," barked Willard. Desk jockey.

The phone rang. "Carbone's been found dead in the camp. Head smashed in. Genitals cut off and placed in mouth."

Someone wanted to make the motive appear sexual. Too obvious.

"Carbone had made a complaint about you. The Delta guys reckon you killed him." Willard was warning me. The army didn't want the case closed.

"You're better off with without me," I told Summer.

"I'll stay."

The phone rang. "General Brubaker's been shot dead." Coomer and Vassell were involved. I just couldn't prove it.

Summer and I flew to France. Too late. My mother had already died. We booked into the George V. "I could use some company."

"Sure thing."

I checked the bill. It gave me all the answers.

"Kramer, Vassell and Coomer were worried Armoured would be cut after the collapse of the Sovs. Carbone was Kramer's lover. He gave Kramer's briefcase to Brubaker, his ex-commander, to make sure Infantry were kept in the loop," I explained.

We flew to California to arrest Coomer and Vassell. They came too quietly.

"I'm missing something." My mind raced.

"I've got it. General Marshall had been hiding in the back of Coomer and Vassell's car. He killed Mrs Kramer, Carbone and Brubaker."

Marshall and I faced each other out on the tank range. No contest. I brought him back unconscious.

"It's been too easy," I said. My mind raced. It was one division of the army against another. I was out of my depth.

"I'm coming with you," Summer insisted.

"Not this time."

She left. I entered Willard's office. "It's just you and me."

"You can't prove a thing."

I put the gun to my temple. "Just kidding," I smiled, and shot him between the eyes. I was alone again.

The digested read ... digested

Stiff prose, stiff stiffs and stiff upper lips

The Final Detail

Harlan Coben

For three weeks Myron Bolitar had been lying on a sun-kissed beach and having great sex. And feeling miserable. He looked up.

"I've got to go," he said to Terese.

On the way back to New York, Win, the handsome millionaire psychopath sidekick, explained why he had turned up. "Clu Haid failed a drugs test and is dead. Esperanza is being held on suspicion of his murder and won't talk to you," he mouthed. "And your clients are leaving your sports agency."

Myron's head spun like Jerry Maguire's. As a former drunk, Clu had been washed up as a pitcher until Myron had got him a last chance with the Yankees. He couldn't have blown it. And why wouldn't his other sidekick, Esperanza, speak to him?

He checked through Clu's phone records. He'd recently been to a transvestite club. "Time for a visit," he thought.

Myron followed the owner into the office where three trannies pulped him.

"What was all that about?"

"Local colour," Win replied. "People expect you to get into sexually ambiguous scrapes."

Myron checked his post and pulled a disk out of a packet. He put it into his computer and an unknown girl briefly appeared before dissolving in blood.

"Time to visit the Yankees."

Sophie Mayor, the billionaire owner of the ball club, let him in. He immediately did a double-take. On the wall was a picture of the same girl who had been on the disk.

"It's my daughter," Sophie explained. "She disappeared ten years ago. Find her." Myron sighed. The plot was already improbable, but he had an inkling things were about to get increasingly absurd.

The phone rang. The transvestite club owner wanted to take him to meet someone. "You didn't expect to see me, did you?" said Billy Lee Palms, removing his blonde wig and brandishing a shotgun. Myron hadn't seen him since that car crash. A shot rang out and Billy Lee fell dead.

"I've no idea what's going on," said Myron.

He checked the phone records. Suddenly it was obvious. Esperanza had been having an affair with Clu's wife. It explained why she wouldn't talk to him. But why would Esperanza kill him?

Myron checked the phone records again. Suddenly it was even more obvious. He went to see Sophie.

"I know everything," he said. "That time 10 years ago when I bribed the police officers to get Clu off a drink-drive charge. It wasn't just Clu, his wife and Billy Lee in the car, was it? Your daughter was there too. But she died and the two men covered it up."

"Very cleffer," Sophie cackled maniacally. "For 10 years I have plotted my revenge. I haff bought ze Yankees only to employ Clu so I could build him up only to throw him on ze scrap heap."

"I'm off to see my mum and dad," Myron replied.

The digested read ... digested

Just an everyday tale of normal law-abiding, cross-dressing psychotic New Yorkers

City of Bones
Michael Connelly

Detective Hieronymus "Harry" Bosch stamped his feet to keep warm. It was tough being a maverick, loner cop as you always got the New Year graveyard shift. A voice crackled over the radio. "A dog's dug up some bones up by Laurel Canyon. Looks like they're human."

Harry called his partner, Jerry Edgar, and made his way up to the woods.

"We're going to need some light," he said. As he reached the patrol car, the back-up showed. It was Julia Brasher, the rookie cop. Harry hurriedly threw a blanket over his torch in the trunk.

"Can I borrow your light?" he asked.

"Is that a Maglite in your pocket or are you just pleased to see me?"

"You know nothing good ever happens to women who fall for loner cops."

"Yeah, but at least you're the hero and I'll get more than a walk-on part."

The pathologist identified the remains as those of a 12-year-old boy who'd been physically beaten throughout his life. "Time of death?" Harry asked.

"Sometime between 1976 and 1984."

Harry hated kid cases, especially ones this old. The chances of catching the perp were almost nil.

"We got a break," said Edgar. "Guy lives nearby got form for child offences."

"Nah," said Harry. "Too obvious."

"Too bad that someone in the department leaked his name to the press and he's topped himself then."

"OK, we got a name for the vic," Harry announced. "His sister rang in. It's Arthur Delacroix. He's been missing since 1980. We're going to check out his former buddy, Johnny Stokes."

Two shots rang out and Julia Brasher slumped to the ground, dying. "I didn't do nothing, man," shouted Johnny.

"I know. She shot herself holstering her gun," said Harry. "Too bad."

Back at the station Harry decided it was time to talk to the vic's father.

"I confess," said Samuel Delacroix.

"You're nicked," cried Edgar.

"Hold on," said Harry. "Too obvious. He's trying to protect the daughter. He thinks she did it. And she's trying to protect him because she thinks he did it."

Harry went back through the records and discovered that Johnny Stokes had been fostered in Laurel Canyon. "He killed him for his skateboard, but we'll never get a conviction now."

Edgar stood over the body of Johnny Stokes. "He was resisting arrest, Harry."

Harry sighed. Maybe it was time to hang up his badge.

The digested read ... digested

After many years of heroic active service with the LAPD, Detective Harry Bosch finally reaches his sell-by date

Cell

Stephen King

Clayton Riddell was bouncing along Boylston Street in Boston when the event that came to be known as the PULSE took place. As is usual at the start of horror fiction, Clay was feeling good. Real good. He was on his way back to Maine to see if he could get back together with his wife, Sharon, and son, Johnny G.

A lady lifted a cell phone to her ear and sank her teeth into the neck of her friend. Blood spurted like a geyser. A man bit the head off a dog, a plane crashed on the next block and the streets ran red.

"Mustn't use the cell phone," Clay said to himself. He ran back to his hotel, dodging the crazies. He found another man – Tom – cowering in the corner and a 15-year old girl – Alice – being attacked by her mother. Clay picked up a metal spike and rammed it through the woman's carotid and left her twitching on the pavement.

"Have you noticed how they seem to go quiet and flock together at dusk?" said Clay, who didn't wonder why no one else in Boston appeared to have realised this. "We can leave the city by night."

The three travelled north, passing countless scenes of unspeakable violence involving mutilated corpses and severed limbs, which they were happy to speak about at length, till they arrived at Gaiten Academy. They were met by a boy called Jordan. "I've got a theory," said the annoyingly precocious Jordan. "The cell phone launched a computer programme that erased the hard drive of everyone's brain."

"That sounds ridiculous enough for me to believe," Clay replied. "Let's torch the flock while they're resting at night."

The flames burnt bright and the stench of burning flesh hung in the air.

"We shouldn't have done that," said Tom.

"Why?"

"I can't tell you as it's just a device to artificially ratchet up the tension for 20 pages."

They all suffered the same nightmare in which the Raggedy Man appeared. "The crazies are psionic," muttered Clay. "They're invading our thoughts and telling us what to do."

"We are sparing you because you are insane," mouthed the Raggedy Man, with a logic that was hard to refute. "Go north."

The four followed the signs to KASHWAK= NO-FO. "It's a place where there's no phone masts," Clay pointed out helpfully, "We'll be safe. But first I've got to find my family."

Alice had a hideous accident and took ten pages to die, but the others pressed on. "It's no good," said Tom. "Sharon is a crazy and Johnny G has been taken prisoner."

"I know," said Clay, "but I still must find him."

"And we'll go with you even though we know it's a trap because the Raggedy Man is making us," Tom answered.

"He's just a pseudopod," Jordan piped up. "There was a virus in the programme and the new crazies are behaving differently. Maybe everyone will eventually reboot to System Restore."

The bomb was ready. Clay dialled the number. The Raggedy Man melted as the Kashwak flock immolated. Tom and Jordan went north to Canada, but Clay still had to find Johnny G. There he was. Or was he? Should he call 911???

The digested read ... digested

A nuisance call

The Constant Gardener

John le Carré

"We've got a problem, Justin," Sandy Woodrow, HM's Head of Chancery in Nairobi, said. "Tessa's been found murdered and her, er, companion, Arnold Bluhm, has gone missing. I'm sorry."

"Good of you to tell me," said Justin.

"All hell's broken loose this end," said Sandy a few hours later as he phoned Bernard Pellegrin, HM's top spook back in London. "The papers are going wild about 'Wife of British diplomat killed by African lover'." I'm not surprised, Sandy thought, recalling his own unrequited passion for Justin's wife.

"Bury the story as best you can," barked the Pellegrin. "Scotland Yard's sending out two detectives and we don't want them poking their noses in. Tessa was a loose cannon and we don't want her and her African doctor's investigation into the Dypraxa TB drug trials jeopardising relations with the Kenyans or the pharmaceutical industry."

"Terribly sorry about Tessa, old chap," soothed the Pellegrin after Justin's recall to London. "Take a bit of time off. Now, you didn't happen to find Tessa's laptop, did you? The police say it's still missing."

"No," replied Justin. "It must have been taken when she was killed."

Bugger them, thought Justin. They all reckon Tessa was having an affair with Arnold, but he was gay; theirs was a meeting of minds, not bodies. But what would the diplomatic service know about truth or integrity? He opened the laptop and started reading Tessa's exposé of the pharma-giants, BBB and KVH. A virus then wiped the hard disk. They were on to him. Never mind. He would continue her crusade regardless.

"You need to speak to Lara Emrich in Saskatchewan," said Birgit, the German activist, at their clandestine rendezvous. "She helped develop Dypraxa."

Hmm. They're still on to me, thought Justin, after receiving a severe beating back at his hotel.

"They rushed the clinical trials," said Emrich. "They were so keen to get the drug on the market they suppressed bad results. Just ask Markus Lorbeer."

Hmm. They're still on to me, thought Justin, after he was followed.

"Yes, you're right," confessed Lorbeer in his Sudanese outpost.

"I'm at my journey's end," thought Justin as the Land Rover pulled up at the spot where Tessa had been killed.

The digested read ... digested

British diplomat loses a wife and finds a conscience as he follows her one-way journey into the dark heart of the pharmaceutical industry

Adam and Eve and Pinch Me

Ruth Rendell

Minty had only had three baths that day. Did her hair need washing
again? Life hadn't been the same since she had received the letter
from Great Western saying that Jock Lewis had been killed in the
Paddington train crash. She had never had a boyfriend before
Jock and now his ghost followed her around the house she had
inherited from Auntie.

Zillah reflected on Jims's offer. Unlimited cash and a home for
her, Eugenie and Jordan in return for a marriage preventing him
being outed as a gay Tory MP.

She'd always known Jerry had faked the letter that said he had
died in the Paddington crash, but surely it meant he wanted nothing
more to do with her? Sod it, she would get married anyway.

Fiona had never been happier. A successful career and now
the gorgeous Jeff Leigh. OK, work life wasn't quite sorted but it
soon would be and he could make the words, "Lend us a couple
of grand, babes," sound terribly sexy. What a shame he didn't
get on with her neighbours, the anorexic Matthew and the clinically
obese Michelle.

"That's it," said Minty to the ghost. "I'm going to have to start
carrying a knife. Follow me to the movies and you get it."

"Just off to another interview," yelled Jeff to Fiona, heading off to
the pictures.

"I warned you," whispered Minty. "Hmm, I never knew ghosts
bled."

"We have reason to believe your husband has been murdered and
that your current marriage is bigamous," said the police officer to

Zillah. "We would also like you and your husband to account for your movements."

"You stupid cow," Jims said. "Now they will find out I was at my lover's house."

"I'm so sorry I told the police you didn't like Jeff," pleaded Fiona to Michelle and Matthew.

"It's all very irritating," agreed Michelle. "But at least Matthew has started eating and I've stopped."

Minty was pleased that Jock's ghost had stopped bothering her. The trouble was that Auntie's had started. "Take that," she said to a homeless derelict.

"Blimey," said the policeman. "We've got another stabbing."

Jims felt relieved Zillah had blabbed about their loveless marriage. He was tired of the sham. He'd give her some dosh, quit parliament and be openly gay.

"Christ," said Lafcadio, Minty's policeman neighbour, after she was arrested for attacking the plumber. "It was her all along. Who would have thought it?"

The digested read ... digested

A large cast of joyless, dim-witted grotesques fail to inspire a moment's compassion or interest

At Risk

Stella Rimington

After 10 years, Liz Carlyle was still the feistiest, quirkiest and most understatedly attractive MI5 operative on the block. Bruno Mackay from MI6 was holding forth in the briefing room. There was something about him she didn't trust: he looked like David Shayler.

"Our team in Pakistan tell us that Faraj Mansoor, an al-Qaida operative, is on his way to Britain," he was saying. "We also hear he will be working with an invisible."

"An invisible is someone who could pass as English without arousing comment," Liz said out loud for no reason other than to fill the reader in. She checked her emails. There was a message from her agent Marzipan; something strange was happening in Norfolk. Could this be the crucial break?

"I had to kill a man at the pick-up," said Faraj. Lucy's blood ran cold. She had been ready for this since she had changed her old, posh name at the Afghan training camp. "It's time to go to the toy shop and the chemist to buy the ingredients for the C4 explosive," she announced in a clumsy sentence, designed to keep the plot moving.

Liz was closing in. The 7.62mm bullet could only have been used by a terrorist, and the Astra on the CCTV had been traced to a rental agency at Waterloo. The driver must be the invisible.

"Check all British women passengers who arrived on the Eurostar," she barked.

"No joy," said her No. 2.

The invisible had to be on the list. Liz cross-checked the names. Jean D'Aubigny. "We thought he was a Frenchman, but she's a posh woman," she shouted, without any shame at such an obvious contrivance. "Now we have to work out why she's here."

Faraj and Jean killed another two people before moving silently through the fens.

"When will you tell me the target?" Jean asked.

"When it's time."

"We must hurry. We are being pursued by a woman and she is getting near."

"Truly you are telepathic."

Bruno and Liz checked out the USAF bases. There was something about the connection between Bruno and the Marwell commander that rang false.

"It's time," said Faraj "The Americans in Marwell killed my fiancée by bombing an Afghan wedding party. At school you were best friends with the base commander's daughter and know the house well."

"You've been holding out on me about about the wedding party," Liz snapped at Bruno, "and Jean knew the base commander's daughter. That's the target."

"Well done, Liz," said her boss, as she recovered in hospital after the blast. "Thanks to you both the terrorists are dead. By the way, Bruno never told us Faraj had been an MI6 agent before the wedding bomb. Keep it up and you'll run MI5 one day."

The digested read ... digested

The former Queen of Spooks lets her imagination get the better of her as she relives her fantasies

Wolves Eat Dogs
Martin Cruz Smith

"It's a straightforward suicide," said Prosecutor Zurin.

Arkady Renko stared into the middle distance. Pasha Ivanov, the head of NoviRus, had been found on the pavement after plunging from the window of his tenth-floor apartment, which was piled high in salt. Nothing was straightforward.

Renko needed a case badly. It was nearly 25 years since he had solved the Gorky Park killings and been acclaimed by *Time* magazine as the thriller detective of the '80s.

"We need to investigate," he said. Ivanov's colleagues Timofeyev and Hoffman glared at him. "This is going to cause trouble," spat Zurin.

"Exactly," Renko smiled.

He phoned the orphanage. He didn't know quite how he had become a part-time carer for Zhenya, a ten-year-old chess genius, but it played well with the readers. It would be the perfect irrelevant leitmotif for the story.

Deep in the wardrobe of Ivanov's apartment, Renko found a dosimeter. The reading went off the scale; the room was radioactive.

Two weeks later, Renko was inside Chernobyl, where Timofeyev's body had been found. "Things are getting better," he said to himself. "No detective has been inside a nuclear disaster zone."

Renko decided it was time to recap. It would help readers who might have been confused by the plot diversions. Ivanov and Timofeyev had worked in the nuclear industry in the '80s. Ivanov had committed suicide because he was dying of radiation poisoning when he jumped. But who put the radioactive salt in his room, and who killed Timofeyev?

Alex Gerasimov was angry. As head of the Chernobyl militia, he wasn't used to outsiders. "Why don't you just go back to Moscow?" he shouted.

"Because there are so many strange vistas to describe, so many vodkas to drink and so many suspects to meet. The Woromays."

And then there was Eva. He knew it was wrong to have an affair with Alex's radioactive ex-wife, but it was hard to resist someone so tragic.

Hoffman had little to say. He had come into Chernobyl unannounced and Renko knew NoviRus security was on to him. "Ivanov just asked me to say the Kaddish at the Jewish cemetery," he said, before Renko had him smuggled out of town.

The Woromays had Renko pinned down. Two shots rang out and the brothers fell dead. Gerasimov turned his gun towards Renko. "You have it all. Ivanov and Timofeyev worked for my father in the ministry in the '80s. They told him Chernobyl was not that bad so he delayed giving the orders to evacuate. Thousands died as a result, so they too have met their punishment. Now you must die."

Another shot was fired. Gerasimov was dead at the hands of yet another peripheral character. All it needed was for Eva to meet Zhenya and the circle was squared.

The digested read ... digested

Renko is back, alive and ticking in Chernobyl

The Minotaur

Barbara Vine

The resemblance to Mrs Cosway was startling, yet I knew it couldn't be her. I turned away. A voice called out. "Kerstin."

She pronounced it Curstin, rather than the correct usage, Shashtin. "Ella?" I asked. Thirty years had passed since that momentous year but the memories were still fresh.

I had come to England in 1968 to reacquaint myself with my lover, Mark. How commonplace this sounds, but at the time it seemed so avant garde. We chose to live apart and I took a job living with the Cosways in a run-down manor house in Essex.

The Cosways reminded me of one of those sinister families I regularly encountered in Victorian fiction. You may think from my language that I am somewhat priggish, but that is far from the case. I just cannot stop myself from writing like Anita Brookner.

The mother, Julia, had an unpleasant tongue. "Look after that useless schizophrenic son of mine," she spat. "Largactil is all he needs."

Three of her daughters, Ida, Ella and Winifred, though middle-aged, were as yet unmarried, and were strangely in her thrall. The youngest daughter, Zorah, was more her own person but still completely out of place in the 1960s.

I have wondered since how much I could have done to avert the tragedy that was to befall – and wondered, also, whether writing those words could generate some much-needed tension in the story – but my duties were not onerous, and I spent much of my time perusing the neglected labyrinthine library that was strangely symbolic yet tangential to the story.

To my surprise, I found John quite normal. He did not seem schizophrenic, but merely mildly autistic.

"I shall be marrying Eric," Winifred declared. This seemed a good match: Eric was the rector, and spinsters are often attracted to the clergy in the Victorian genre.

"None of this seems quite real to me," Mark said one weekend, as I told him of Julia's affair with the village doctor. So I left him and took up with the organist's son.

The arrival of the bohemian Felix changed everything, and Ella secretly told me she was in love. But it was when I chanced upon Winifred also making secret assignations with Felix that a chill ran through me.

Should I have done more to stop it? How can you prevent the predictability of the second-rate Victorian pastiche?

I later discovered the whole village knew all the family secrets, but by then it was too late. Winifred was dead. "It was that mad son of mine," yelled Julia.

I informed the police this could not be. Thereafter Ida and Julia accused one another, and the investigation only ended when Julia died in a manor house fire reminiscent of *Jane Eyre*.

My mind returned to the present. "So John is all right?" "Yes," said Ella, "and I married the rector."

The digested read ... digested

Kerstin picks up the threads to find a load of old bull

The digested read ...

Eurotrash

Crabwalk

Gunter Grass

You ask why Germans have no sense of humour. I'll tell you. But first I will walk sideways, crablike, to the truth.

I need to settle my own historical accounts. I know I have messed up but it is sheer accident I am here at all, that Mother – I cannot bring myself to use the possessive "my" – was nine months pregnant at the time.

It started when I bought a computer and started surfing the net. I flicked from chatroom to chatroom, listening to neo-Nazis, before I came to www.blutzeuge.de, the Comrades of Schwerin.

Two men. Wilhelm Gustloff, the Nazi *Landesgruppen-Leiter*, and David Frankfurter, the Jew who killed him. Both had come alive in the chatroom. Gustloff had become a martyr when he was murdered on January 30, 1936, and the Nazis named a cruise ship after him. Mother and her parents had their best holiday on the *Gustloff*.

After the war, mother stayed on in the East. She never quite lost her love of the Nazis. She sent me to live in the West just before the wall went up. "Tell this man he's your father," she said. "He'll give you money." I got the money. I never discovered my father.

I became a journalist, a poor one. I met a woman called Gabi, we had a son, Konrad, and she left me. Mother adored Konrad.

I must go sideways once more. For mother, her defining event was the sinking of the *Gustloff*. She was just 18 and was fleeing on board the *Gustloff*, which had become a refugee ship. Nine thousand died when it was sunk by a Russian submarine. Only a few survived. "You were born as the ship sank," she used to tell me, though this was a lie. I was born on the rescue boat.

"Tell me," she would say. "Why have we destroyed the memorial to the *Gustloff* that went up before the war? Why should we remember instead the Jew and the submarine commander?"

In the chatrooms, my suspicions grew. The voice of Wilhelm was Konrad, infected by his grandmother. This was confirmed when Konrad agreed to meet the voice of David in person. They visited the sites in Schwerin and then Konny killed him. "It is vengeance," he said.

The papers lost interest in the case when they discovered that David was not a Jew. He was Wolfgang Stremplin. "Maybe he wouldn't have been so passionate had we talked more of the Nazis at home," his parents told me. "Maybe Konny would not have been so full of hatred if I had been a better parent, too," I replied. Ach, German angst.

Konny was sent to prison. At first he showed no signs of repentance, then one day I visited him and saw he had thrown out all his Nazi cuttings. That night I went home and logged on. There was a site dedicated to Konrad, the hatred he had brought. It never ends.

The digested read ... digested

The existential fulfilment of the thousand-year Reich

Francesco's Italy

Francesco da Mosto

Italy is a land of contrasts. And I am a man of cliché. For me, the family is everything. I was born in Venice – but for the last four generations the Da Mostos have taken their brides from elsewhere. My mother is Sicilian. So the blood of all Italy courses through my veins, and this is my story of my travels. Like me, it is small but perfectly formed.

Long before the birth of the Most Serene Republic of Venice, a distant ancestor of my family, the nobleman Titus Mustius, was a prominent citizen of Padua, so it was in that direction I headed first in my Alfa Spider to witness the extraordinary genius of Giotto first hand. From there, I pass through Vicenza – was Palladio too good, I sometimes wonder – and Verona to stay on the shores of Lake Garda, which enjoys a mild climate. Here I reread Catullus's rapturous, erotic love poems to his mistress Lesbia.

Heading south across the Po, we pass through Bologna and Milan to the hinterland of Liguria. Here my family has another house; it stands on the hill of Sant' Ilario and overlooks the sea. How well I remember waiting until lots of girls were swooning in delight before diving into the sea when I was young!

When 20 years ago, wearing military uniform topped with the plumed hat of the Alpine regiment, I made my way to Pisa, I thought about the bloody battle of the Arno. It was sobering to reflect upon the proximity of beauty to tragedy, but for me Tuscany is still essentially a large house in the hills where my cousin, la bella Orsetta, and I were drawn into a tightly woven net as the Angelus bell chimed nearby.

Even today I am overwhelmed by Florence, and Siena is still the embodiment of civic pride. But it is Assisi, whose patron saint was named after me, where my soul finds gentle repose. Reluctantly I move south to Rome – *la citta eterna*, the birthplace of modern history – though traffic remains a perennial problem. In ancient Rome there were 40 varieties of pear tree; today it is easier to find a pizza!

Italian history has not always been covered in glory. The Inquisition and the fascist dictatorship of Mussolini were not our finest hours, but I prefer to dwell on the works of Michelangelo and Caravaggio, the music of Puccini and Gesualdo and the musky scent of grapes maturing on a Tuscan vine.

The region of Puglia, the "heel" of Italy, is a land of castles and horses. Or so my picture book tells me. My more refined sensibilities turn more to Goethe and Alexander the Great, though why this should be I am not entirely sure. Perhaps it is because I am looking up towards Vesuvius from my Neapolitan palazzo.

As I cross the turbulent Strait of Messina, within a bowshot of Scylla and Charybdis, I sense I am reaching my journey's end. I make my way up to the ancient amphitheatre of Taormina and gaze out towards the burning fires of Etna, before heading west to Palermo. It was here that my mother, the most beautiful woman who ever lived, was born, and as I walk up the grand double flight of the marble stairs that led to her frescoed salon, I feel her spirit come alive. For some, Sicily is the cradle of civilisation; for me it is a return to the womb.

The digested read ... digested

Too little, too latte

Purity of Blood

Arturo Pérez-Reverte

Chief Constable Martin Saldana told us about the *duena* who had been found strangled in her sedan chair that afternoon by the church of San Gines. Or to be more precise he told Captain Alatriste. You may remember, Your Mercies, the two men were present on that same attack on the walls of Ostend some 20 years ago. Alatriste fingered his sword. "Madrid has become too dangerous," he said. "I'm thinking of returning to my old *tercio*."

Your Mercies, please indulge me when I tell you that the Spain of Phillip IV had become a corrupt and immoral society, and that clipped, inconsequential dialogue had become the order of the day. Out of the corner of my eye, I spotted the great poet don Francisco de Quevedo, the equal to Cervantes. Little did I know how our lives would change.

"I have a favour to ask," said Don Francisco.

Alatriste, a man never given to many words, merely grunted. He could not refuse.

While Alatriste was glum and terse

Quevedo oft did speak in verse

"Go outside, Inigo," the Captain said to me, though I merely hid when don Francisco introduced an elderly man, Don Vicente de la Cruz, and his two sons. "My daughter, Elvira, has been taken by a duena and is being held in the convent of La Adoracion," he said, "where Padre Coroado treats the novices as his seraglio. We cannot free her, though, for fear the Padre will expose our Jewish blood."

Your Mercies, please forgive me when I say that the Church was most cruel and unholy at this time. Never trust a man who only reads one book.

Alatriste stroked his melancholy moustache. "There will be bloodshed."

As we unlocked the convent's garden door, we were ambushed on all sides by armed men. Alatriste bade me flee while his sword ran red with rivers of blood. I hurried past the dying Don Vicente straight on to the blade of Alatriste's greatest enemy, Gualterio Malatesta.

As events become more torrid

So the rhyme becomes more florid

"It gives me little pleasure to hand you over to the Inquisition," said Malatesta. But turn me in, Your Mercies, he did. And though at 13 years old I was too young for the rack, I was whipped mercilessly, but I am proud to say that never once did I betray my master, Alatriste.

"*Pardiez*. We have been undone. Alquezar has used us to discredit the convent and to settle his account with me," growled Alatriste in the longest sentence he ever uttered. "But we must save Inigo."

I watched Elvira burn as I awaited my own sentence at the *auto-da-fé*. Your Mercies, I tell you that I never saw Don Francisco approach Alquezar with a document in the royal box.

We have the proof that you're a Jew

Release the boy, or I'll run you through

Neither did I see Alatriste draw his dagger in the plaza, leaving two henchmen to rot in hell, and Malatesta himself reeling from his wounds.

Your Mercies, as I enjoyed my freedom, Alatriste hunted Malatesta to his rooms. "Finish me off," Malatesta cried, as the Captain held a pistol to his head. But Alatriste just turned and laughed.

The digested read ... digested

The One Musketeer

The Possibility of an Island

Michel Houellebecq

Daniel 1,1: I get so tired writing comic sketches about gays, blacks, Jews and Muslims these days. But being thought to be avant garde has its advantages; people take you seriously and pay you shed loads of cash for any old tosh. And you get lots of pussy, too.

Daniel 24,1: Look at those savages in the distance. They are humans. I sit alone in my fenced-off compound sending the odd email to Marie 22.

I am not happy, I am not sad
I never cry and I'm never bad

Daniel 1, 2: I don't know why I married my first wife and I didn't care when my son committed suicide. That's how shocking I am. I met Isabelle when she came to interview me after the success of *We Prefer the Palestinian Orgy Sluts*. She was OK; her tits didn't sag and I felt almost affectionate towards her. We stayed together for a while in a house I had bought in Spain with my many million euros.

Daniel 24, 2: I am neo-human. I sit here with Fox, reflecting aimlessly on our previous incarnations.

I'm even deep
When I'm asleep

Daniel 1, 3: Isabelle aged badly and I grew tired of her. I acquired a dog I called Fox, who was much better company. One morning some neighbours invited me to join the Elohim sect. Weighed down by my professional ennui I was naturally sceptical, but the prospect of free love and everlasting life was undeniably attractive.

Daniel 24, 3: Marie 22 sent me an email.

My breasts are low
It's time to go

She is about to become Marie 23.

Daniel 1, 4: With Esther I thought I had discovered happiness. Just looking at her 22-year-old body gave me a hard-on and she willingly let me fuck her in every orifice.

Daniel 25, 1: Daniel 24 has had enough, The Supreme Sister has called him.

Daniel 1, 5: Esther left me as I knew she would, but my Fourierist principles had drawn me ever closer to the Elohim. I had even taken to writing doggerel.

Just one push
On a friendly bush

Vincent had replaced the Prophet and he was convinced the time of human cloning was drawing ever nearer.

Daniel 25, 2: It was around this time that the early leaders pioneered a genetic mutation of autotrophism, allowing the new species to survive on minerals and water.

Daniel 1, 6: Sometimes I think I overstated my despair; though not that of my readers. I chose to visit Isabelle. "I still love you," she said, before committing suicide.

Daniel 25, 3: Marie 23 has escaped to live with the savages. I read Spinoza.

Daniel 1, 7: Occasionally my cock showed signs of life, but I had come to realise that happiness was the preserve of the young. Vincent suggested that Fox and I should have our DNA copied. "It is time for you to commit suicide," he said. "You will be an example for millions of others." I sent a last poem to Esther.

You are in clover
But my life is over

Daniel 25, 4: I'm tired of feeling nothing. I break out. I smell the pestilential ordure between a savage's legs and make for the hills. I will die. I am finally alive.

The digested read ... digested

25 Daniels don't give a damn. And neither will you

North
Americana

A Summer Crossing

Truman Capote

"You are a mystery, my dear," Lucy McNeil said, and her daughter Grady smiled indulgently. "Why, I guess I am a little perverse," she replied.

"Well, I will worry about you," her mother continued. "Seventeen is very young to stay on your own in New York. But I shall bring you back the finest ballgown for your society debut."

"I can't think why Grady doesn't want to go to Europe with you," snapped Apple who, being eight years the older, was by far the more sensible of the McNeil sisters.

But Grady could not tell the truth. Be proud, she said to herself, and fly your pennant high above and in the wind.

A voice echoed in the hall. "Hello McNeil." It could only be Grady's friend, Peter Bell, and the pair giggled and sipped champagne as her parents prepared to depart. Lucy looked on kindly as Peter was from a well-to-do family.

"I wish that you could love me as I love you," Peter sighed. Poor Peter, Grady thought. How little he knows me. Perhaps one day I can tell him.

Grady strolled to the Broadway parking lot. She looked down at the young man. "Light me a cigarette," he growled.

Clyde Manzer was not the first lover she had ever known, but he was the first with whom she had been truly smitten. When they kissed, she could sense a raw, mumbling power.

"I love you," Grady mewed. Clyde said nothing. Since the war had ended, his life had been a disappointment. Was working in a parking lot the best he could expect? He knew the affair with Grady

McNeil was going nowhere. He was down-at-heel and had friends called Mink and Gump. Worst of all, he was Jewish.

"I don't care if you're Jewish," Grady cried. "Come back to my Fifth Avenue apartment and I'll bake you a cake."

Clyde buttoned his flies and switched on the ball game. "I love you so much," Grady pleaded as she lay naked on the bed. "Why can you not love me?" Ah, what the hell, thought Clyde, and they were married in secret that afternoon.

Grady languished alone in the New York heatwave. She knew why she was so reluctant to tell her family about the wedding, but why could Clyde not tell his? They were such a sweet Jewish family and she felt so welcome. And why did Clyde spend so little time with her? How lucky she was to still have Peter as a friend, because otherwise she would never go out at all.

The apartment had been empty for days and Clyde was getting curious. "I believe she's visiting her sister in the Hamptons," the valet said.

"Why Grady," said Apple. "There's this man at the door. He says he's your husband. Tell me it's not true."

"But it is," wailed Grady. "And I'm 16 weeks pregnant. Mother and Father return next week. Whatever shall I do?"

"I'm taking you home," growled Clyde.

"Oh no you don't," said Peter.

The two men grappled in the back of the Buick as Grady drove over the Queensboro Bridge while inhaling deeply on a reefer.

"Damn it, you'll kill us all."

And not a moment too soon, thought the reader.

The digested read ... digested

Adolescent fumblings – on and off the page

Hey Nostradamus!

Douglas Coupland

Cheryl, 1988

When you're a 16-year-old girl with the surname Anyway, you know you're going to wind up dead. How come every hip word-slinger in town has to include a high-school massacre these days?

Here's my story, Anyway. I'd been part of this God squad Youth Alive! when I met Jason. He begged me to go to bed with him, but I refused unless we got married. So we went off to Las Vegas and tied the knot without telling anyone. The day I died we had a row when I told him I was pregnant. We were going to make up but these three geeks from 12th grade came into the canteen as if on a duck shoot. They took out a load of kids before Jason came in. He killed one of the geeks trying to save me, but it was too late. Before I died, I was doodling in my book, like you do, God is Nowhere, God is Now Here. People made a lot of that after I died, but it meant nothing.

Jason, 1999

I'm sitting here with a beer, going nowhere. My life stopped when Cheryl died. Did you know we were married? At first I was a hero, but my dad, Reg, just said I had murder in my heart. He's a fucking religious nutcase. I've not spoken to him since. My Mum broke his leg and left him. She's a drunk but she has her good days.

The police got to wondering if maybe I was in with the three geeks and the Alivers! Did me no favours, either. By the time people realised I was innocent, the damage had been done. My brother

Kent – the family good-guy – got totalled in a crash. His wife, Barb, made me get her pregnant and now she's got twins. What's all that about? I had a blackout and found this guy called Yorgo chasing me with a gun. I never found out why. I could have killed him, but decided not to. That's redemption of a sort, I guess.

Heather, 2002
When I met Jason it was like we were soul mates. We knew what each other was going to say before we said it. He's been missing a while now. He talked about some weird Russian, but he was happy. There's no way he would leave me.

I got a call from a psychic called Allison. "I'm a shit psychic," she said. "But I have a message: 'The cat sat on the mat.'" It was our phrase. I got to paying her money for more and more messages, but eventually I found out that Jason had given her all these messages to pass on to me in case he disappeared. Where's the God in that?

Reg, 2003
You thought I was a bigot, didn't you, Jason? Well I was. But I got a new girlfriend. I've always loved you. I'm sorry I didn't think you were innocent. But I do now. And you will get this letter. My son is coming home!

The digested read ... digested
Get out of this one, God

Lunar Park
Bret Easton Ellis

You do an awfully good impression of yourself. This is the first line of *Lunar Park*. It's meant to be a return to form. As anyone familiar with my work will know, things had been getting steadily out of hand after my first book, *Less Than Zero*. Everything happened ridiculously easily. Within four months of publication, I was wealthy, insanely famous and I had escaped my father.

Everyone loved me; the more I tried to gross people out with drugs, sex and gratuitous violence, the more half-witted readers lapped it up. No stylistic tic was too pretentious for the gullible literati. Along the way, my father died in 1992, I had a son with a B-movie actress, Jayne Dennis – though for a long time I denied this – and I did a lot of drugs. But recently I became aware that I wanted more than just being richer and more famous than anyone else in America. So I moved back in with Jayne and my son, Robby, and her daughter, Sarah.

"You do an awfully good impression of yourself," Jayne said pointedly when I told her I was going as me to our Halloween party. I took an eight-ball of coke before going to the Camden campus to see one of my students, Aimée Light. "Tell me about *American Psycho*," she whispered, pulling me close like the cock-tease she was.

Jayne refused to talk to me the next morning. She knew I'd gone missing during the party. I didn't care. Sure I had been stoned, but it had been the guy I had caught out of the corner of my eye in the White Merc who had freaked me out. Later that day, Aimée introduced me to a guy called Clayton. Only later did I realise he was the guy in the Merc. And he looked like Patrick Bateman in *American Psycho*.

For the next few days, I tried to act normal. I wanted to be a father to Robby and husband to Jayne, but my desire not to let my readers down won through. I didn't get six-figure advances for suburban normality; my readers wanted drugs, violence and weirdness. I took some bumps of coke, namedropped the Jayster and started to freak out when several boys went missing and Sarah's fluffy-toy Terby turned killer.

Detective Kimball called. There was someone out there doing *American Psycho* copycat killings and Aimée Light was missing. "You're stoned," said Jayne, but I knew I was really just another tricksy, unreliable narrator. The Terby was trying to kill the kids, the White Merc flashed in and out of view, Clayton lurked in the distance – his face alternating between that of Patrick Bateman and my father.

I called in the ghostbusters. "We've got demons here," said Miller. But the real answer was closer to home. Kimball was another of my creations. Everything – as it always had done – revolved around me. My fiction had come to life and I needed a resolution. I drank some vodka. That wasn't it. I needed to scatter my father's ashes.

Robby ran off to join the lost boys. There just wasn't enough room for both of us on the page – though I later thought I saw someone who might have been him who also looked a bit like Clayton.

The digested read ... digested

Bret plays with himself but remains rather limp

Our Lady of the Forest

David Guterson

The girl went in to the forest to collect mushrooms, though she may
have stopped to smoke a joint or take some antihistamines. And
she later told Father Collins she twice stopped to masturbate. The
papers reported that her name was Ann Holmes, a waif-like 16-
year-old who had been sexually abused by her stepfather but now
lived alone in North Fork forest in Oregon.

"The Virgin Mary has come to me," said Ann dreamily. "She wants
us to build a church in the forest."

Carolyn Greer was also a stereotype. She was a plump, dope-
smoking mushroom picker with an eye on the main chance and
keen to befriend Ann. "Let's go back to the forest to see if the
apparition returns."

"Oh look, there's the Virgin Mary again," sighed Ann. "I don't feel
very well. I think I've got a temperature."

The following day several more people joined them. By the end
of the week more than a thousand people were camped out in
the forest.

"The Blessed Mother still wants us to build a church," Ann cried.
"Give me some Tylenol, I'm still not well."

Father Collins was another stereotype. He was riven with self-
doubt over the works of Aquinas and Saint Augustine and
predisposed to onanism. "Am I really bad?" he intoned, while
self-flagellating.

Tom Cross had appeared in dozens of Bruce Springsteen songs:
a blue-collar worker, driven to despair by the economy and a loveless
marriage. "I am a bad, bad man," he yelled. "My son uz paralysed

because of ma hatred. I called him a pussy and a tree fell on him while we wuz out loggin'."

"We must build that church, Father," Ann pleaded. "But I am not baptised. I will not be saved."

"You're looking a bit peaky," replied Father Collins, trying to get a glimpse of her underwear. "Are you sure you're not on drugs?"

"Of course, she's on drugs," snapped Father Butler, the bishop's delegate and yet another lazily drawn character. "She is not part of God's plan like Sister Catherine Laboure."

"You're so knowledgeable," said Father Collins. "This must be literary fiction."

"See how the holy water flows," Ann whispered slowly. "I'm feeling worse and worse."

"Hang on in there," said Carolyn. "The crowd is throwing money at us."

"I want some of that water to cure ma son," yelled Tom.

"Step away from that woman," shouted Carolyn, who had just stuffed $10,000 into her duffel bag.

"The church," groaned Ann, as she slumped to the floor.

Father Collins looked around the nave. His was now the finest church in Oregon. There in the sacristy, Tom prepared the wafers for the first communion. Carolyn rushed in. "I killed her. I was going to steal the money."

"Calm yourself. She died of a fever," Father Collins replied, making a sign of the cross. "Blessed are the gullible· for they shall buy this book."

The digested read ... digested

Feeble US whimsy that splutters on a wing and a prayer

Adverbs

Daniel Handler

Love was in the air, so both of us walked through love on the way to the corner.

"Your dad died two weeks ago and you only told me today," said Andrea. "I guess you must be in shock but it is very, very, very, very difficult."

"He wasn't really my dad," I replied, getting into a cab and leaving her behind. I glanced at the driver and saw his name was Peter. "I love you, Peter."

Money money money money money. Let no one say it doesn't have a place in a love story. Helena bought a carton of milk for $100,000. "You've written a novel," said her husband, David. "I can get you a teaching job with an old girlfriend, Andrea, in San Francisco."

"Tell your class about magpies," Andrea whispered.

"I remember a lover called Keith," I said. "He had a big penis, but maybe he wasn't real."

Two detectives walked into the diner and showed Andrea and Mike a photo. "Have you seen this woman?"

"It's Gladys," Mike replied.

"Kaatu, kaatu, maka I am the Snow Queen the Snow Queen," Gladys said in a mysterious howl, before flying away.

After San Francisco had been struck by the volcanic catastrophe, Eddie and Mike stood high on the hill. Was this love? In the novel she might have been in her underwear. But she wasn't, so she wasn't.

Adam and Eddie went into the forest forest forest to have sex. They were interrupted by Eddie's former lover Tomas. "Please help my friend Steven, who has fallen," Tomas pleaded.

Eddie and Steven stayed behind. "I think we should have sex sex sex," he said. "I have a 10in penis."

"That is the oldest line in the book." But which book? And should they?

"Is this a good time?" Steven asked.

"I don't know," said Allison. "I was dreaming of a boyfriend called Hank Hayrick who turned out to be a ghost."

"But what about Joe?"

This is the moment you've been expecting as I'm so drearily post-modern I have to appear in my own work. It's me Daniel Handler aka Lemony Snicket, though you probably guessed that as no one in their right mind would have published this tosh unless I had sold gazillions of children's books. Don't worry if you can't keep up with the plot or the people. They are just unimportant nouns. It's the way they do things, the adverbs adverbs adverbs that count. Though adverb is of course a noun.

Keith, Allison, Mike, Andrea and Andrea – maybe there are two Andreas, who cares? – dream and slide between one another. Helena spends another $5m on dinner and rubs her tummy. Often, judgmentally, symbolically. Is she pregnant?

In another part of town, Joe gets out of a cab. "You've arrived," says the lady.

And this is the moment Daniel hasn't been expecting, the moment the Digested Read climbs into his novel. "Thank you for waving your literary nob," said John. "Shame it's so small."

The digested read ... digested

A Series of Unreadable Events

The Fourth Hand

John Irving

Imagine a young man on his way to a 30-second appointment with destiny.

That man was Patrick Wallingford, a TV reporter in India to cover the trapeze disaster. It was feeding day at the circus and the meat wallahs were distracted by the German girl without a bra. Patrick knew she was German because he had slept with her the night before, in his final act of acquiescence to women, which precipitated his divorce from Marilyn. Anyway, one of the lions grew testy at the delay. It flicked out a paw, grabbed Patrick's left wrist and bit his hand off.

Patrick was less than happy that the event was broadcast around the world; it wasn't the fame or the "Lion Guy" tag that bothered him so much as the fact that so many people had seen him wet his pants. Still, fame had its advantages.

The new hand turned up via www.needahand.com. Mrs Clause from Wisconsin had volunteered her husband Otto's hand. He was still alive. But within months the ethical problems had disappeared as he had died mysteriously.

"We have the right hand for you," Dr Zajac said. "But it's the left one," pleaded Patrick. Zajac ignored him. "There's a condition that the donor's family wants visitation rights."

Doris Clause took off her pants and knickers and mounted Patrick. "Otto and I always wanted a baby," she whispered. "Make me pregnant."

Patrick spent weekends visiting Doris and baby Otto, but he never became fully attached to his new hand. Zajac removed the body part. "You did try to keep Otto's hand alive," added Doris.

Patrick may have lost a hand twice, but he had gained a soul. The sensationalisation of the TV news no longer motivated him. He had tried hard, if unsuccessfully to fight off Mary, his producer, and Angie, the make-up girl. But it was Doris and baby Otto he wanted. "Will you marry me?" he asked. "I'll think about it," she said. "Come to the Packers game on November 1."

"We need you in Long Island," said Mary. "I'm going to Green Bay."

"You're fired."

"There's your good hand and the two that you've lost," whispered Doris, "and then there's your fourth." She grabbed the stump and squeezed it between her thighs, where he felt his missing fingers come back to life. "This is the one that will never forget me."

The digested read ... digested

A knockabout comedy that turns deceptively and disarmingly into a hymn of redemptive love

Love Me

Garrison Keillor

My name's Larry Wyler. Once I was young and virtually indestructible: now I'm an old married guy living in St Paul, Minnesota. The people next door don't know I'm a famous former author and that I write the agony-aunt column, Mr Blue, for the *Minneapolis Star Journal*.

I've behaved pretty badly over the years. When my novel, *Spacious Skies,* became an unexpected success, I left my wife, Iris, and took a shot at fame. The *New Yorker* asked me to write for them, I had dozens of affairs and hung out with John Updike and William Shawn. Iris almost divorced me, but couldn't quite make the break: I guess she loved me.

Thing is, I never wrote a word for the *New Yorker.* Writer's block. My second novel bombed, and that was that. I was grateful for Mr Blue. Six years on, I ended up accidentally killing the *New Yorker's* owner, and came back to St Paul. And that's basically the entire story in three pages: it's a favour to the reviewers – save them having to read the next 269.

So here we go, back to the beginning. Iris and I met at university: we fell in love, she became a social worker and I became a writer. I didn't have much – well, any – success at first, but then *Spacious Skies* became a best-seller, and I got a letter from William Shawn, the *New Yorker* editor, asking me to write for him.

Garrison here. Look, I'm sorry. I know you were thinking that I couldn't just repeat myself, but I can't help it. I'm stuck. I'm hoping the critics will be dumb enough to pass it off as comic literary irony, but believe me it isn't. I've just reached that point so many writers reach: I now only hang out with writers so I've no idea how anyone else lives any more. I can only write about writing, and now I've written myself into such a cul-de-sac I have writer's block.

It's Larry again. Before long, I was struck by writer's block. My second novel was panned and Shawn described my few feeble attempts as girly. Still, I had a lot of affairs. The call from the *Star Journal* was a godsend. It brought in $1,200 a week and I enjoyed dispensing advice.

Mr Blue was a godsend to me, Garry, too.

Dear Mr Blue, I haven't written a word for ten days and I'm getting anxious.

Dear Anxious, Don't worry. You're reaching your contractual word count anyway.

Do you see what I mean? You can fill up the pages with any number of dull problems and you've knocked off half the book.

Back to me. John Updike told me I had to kill the Mafia boss who owned the *New Yorker*. So I did, sort of accidentally. Then I went back to St Paul and after a short while I moved back in with Iris. And that's it really.

Are you really still reading this stuff? Well, I'm not writing it any more.

The digested read ... digested

Writer writing about writer writing about writer's block. If only

No Country for Old Men

Cormac McCarthy

Moss fingered the heavy-barreled .270 on a '98 Mauser action with a laminated walnut and maple stock. He glassed the Texan desert with a pair of 12 power German binoculars. There were men lying on the ground beside two trucks.

Agua, said the one man still alive. An H&K on his lap and an exit wound in his throat.

Aint got no water.

Moss checked the back of the truck. Packets of a brown powder and a valise. He flipped the catch. $2.4m. He left the powder, took the valise and headed home. This kind of changed everthing.

Where you been?

You dont need to know, Carla Jean.

He woke at 1.06. Theres something I gotta do.

What is it?

You dont need to know.

Moss headed back to the trucks. The Mexican was dead. Shots from a sawn-off shotgun rang out and Moss headed for the road, blood streaming from his back.

I dont know when things started getting nasty roun here. Folks say it was after Vietnam but I reckon it started before that.

Sheriff Bell surveyed the eight bodies bloating in the sun. Things are gonna get tough for Moss and Carla Jean, he reckoned.

Moss checked the curtains at the motel. He had company. He lifted the air vent. Two Mexicans pooling blood and the money in the corner. He retrieved the money, removed the transponder and a blast took him in the back. He fired the sawn-off and limped downtown. He was a dead man. Shots from a machine-pistol rang out and four Mexicans lay dying. A reprieve.

Chigurh was a patient man. He stitched his wounds. He hadn't got the money yet. But he would. Too bad those Mexicans got in the way. But four less to deal with later.

The man called Wells.

Find me the money and get Chigurh.

Wells tracked Moss to the hospital.

Wheres the money?

Safe.

You wont be. Call me.

Chigurh cornered Wells.

How does a man decide in what order to abandon his life?

Wells shrugged and the bullet blew away his forehead.

Chigurh went to the man

You sent Wells to kill me. Now you gonna die.

He fired into the carotid as his phone rang.

It's too late, Moss. But you can save your wife.

Not if I get you first.

Chigurh crept up on Moss. Time to die.

Bell shrugged as he saw the putrefying corpse. What could he tell Carla Jean?

You know who I am?

Carla Jean nodded.

I promised your husband I'd kill you and I keep my promises. You stay settin there. He aimed carefully and fired.

My granddaddy was a sheriff and I was proud to be a sheriff. But I reckon I've had enough.

There was no sign of Chigurh. This country could kill you in a heartbeat.

The digested read ... digested

Once Upon a Time in the West

Everyman

Philip Roth

Around the grave in the rundown cemetery were a few of his former advertising colleagues, some people who had driven up from the Starfish Beach retirement village, his elder brother, Howie, his second wife, Phoebe, his two sons, Lonny and Randy and his daughter, Nancy.

"This is how it turns out. There's nothing more we can do, Dad," said Nancy, throwing some dirt on to the top of the coffin. The day before the surgery, he had remembered going into hospital as a boy for a hernia operation and how the boy in the next bed had died. But this was not the first death he had known; the year before he had found a German submariner washed up on the shore. "It happens," his father had said.

He had got married and divorced – he couldn't blame Lonny and Randy for hating him – and he had remarried. He had been happy with Phoebe and Nancy was adorable, but really the next most interesting event in his life had been when he had had life-threatening surgery at the age of 31 on a burst appendix.

Twenty-two years of excellent health passed and then the EKG showed radical changes in his heart that indicated severe occlusion of his major coronary arteries. It was touch and go whether he would make it. By now he had moved on to his third wife, but she had no taste for a crisis so by the time he recovered he went home alone.

He fell in love with his nurse – a not uncommon experience – and she moved in with him after his father died. The night of the funeral he could almost taste the dirt finding its way into his father's mouth and choking him.

For the next nine years his health remained disappointingly stable, but then in 1998 his blood pressure began to mount and the doctors diagnosed an obstruction of the renal artery and he was admitted to hospital for angioplasty. Again his luck held, and he returned home to his one real pleasure – revising his will.

After 9/11 he moved out to Starfish Beach where he might have enjoyed himself teaching painting classes. But fortunately enough of his elderly students were dying of cancer and his star pupil overdosed on sleeping tablets to save him from any feelings of positivity.

From time to time, he cast his mind back to his wives, his mistresses and his former job. He had had some good sex and some bad sex and his career had been better than average, but all it really amounted to was a diversion between hospital visits. And in the last seven years of his life, he was pleased to note that he had needed major surgery at least once every twelve months. A stent here, a stent there: what more could one ask? How could he have ever envied Howie his good health?

He had been going to ask Nancy if he could move in with her, but just as he was about to call, she had phoned to say that her mother had had a stroke and would be moving in instead. "I'm sorry to hear that," he had said before phoning the widow of his former boss and an old friend who had terminal cancer to offer his condolences. He had then befriended a grave digger, before entering hospital for surgery on his right carotid artery. This time there was no coming back.

The digested read ... digested

Life's a bitch and then you die

The Amateur Marriage

Anne Tyler

Everyone said Michael and Pauline were a perfect couple from the moment they met.

"Hello Michael," said Pauline, as she walked into Anton's hardware shop the day after Pearl Harbor.

"Aw, shucks," Michael blushed. "I'm joining the army. We'll write every day."

* * *

Pauline sometimes thought Michael was a bit of a bore. And she couldn't help sometimes wishing the bullet that had invalided him out of the army had struck higher. If only she had known how much the readers agreed.

* * *

Lindy, George and Karen played in the drive of their new home in the Baltimore suburbs. "Aw shucks," said Michael after finishing the accounts, "it's time for our Saturday night lovemaking." Pauline thought of her stolen kisses with the neighbour.

* * *

Lindy was 17 and had gone missing before. "Aw shucks," Michael said. "I'll call the police in three hours, 12 minutes and seven seconds."

As the days turned into months, Michael and Pauline got used to the fact that Lindy was not coming back. Some days they didn't even think of her: on others Michael wondered how much he was saving by not having to pay for her food.

* * *

"I got a call from San Francisco," Pauline said. "Lindy's in an institution and she's left her child with a stranger. We need to go there."

"We want to see Lindy," demanded Michael and Pauline at the refuge.

"You can't," said Destiny.

"OK," said Pauline.

"Aw shucks," mumbled Michael.

"Perhaps we should pick up Lindy's son first."

* * *

Pagan settled in well with Michael and Pauline. He never asked about his mother and they never talked about her. Pauline reckoned that for all Michael's faults, they still had a happy marriage.

* * *

"Happy 30th wedding anniversary, darling."

"I'm leaving," Michael shouted.

Pauline felt sure Michael would return but as the days turned into months, she learned to live without him. They shared custody of Pagan.

* * *

Michael felt a strange affinity for Anna. After a year they married. They were happy, though Anna did wonder why Michael was so boring.

* * *

George was wondering, but not too much, how his father had coped after Pauline died in a car crash, when the doorbell rang. It was Lindy.

"Why did you leave 25 years ago?"

"I dunno. Does Pagan want to see me?"

"Not really," said Pagan.

* * *

Michael was now in his 80s. Anna was being a bit difficult and he was starting to think Pauline hadn't been so bad after all.

The digested read ... digested

The life less considered

The digested read ...

Oedipal reads

Father Figure

Ann Widdecombe

Jason sighed. It was tough being a history teacher at Somerset's worst-performing secondary school. Still, he mused, it would soon be time to go home to his gorgeous wife, Kat, and his two adorable children, Jake and Leah.

As he pulled into the drive, Jason was surprised that no lights were on. He walked through the door and felt a cold shudder run down his spine as he spotted a note on the table. "I'm leaving you and I'm taking the kids," it read. He called Kat's mobile. "Look," she said. "There's no one else involved. It's just that you're too boring."

"How can you do something like this with so little explanation?" he wailed.

"Because I'm an utterly one-dimensional character whose only purpose is to give you a hard time."

Jason sought out Ed Deacon, whose wife had left him a year earlier.

"I'm living in a cardboard box and I'm completely broke," Ed moaned. "I never get to see the kids at all."

The solicitor confirmed Ed's predictions. "Your wife can do what she likes," he said. "You'll be lucky if the kids even recognise you within a couple of years."

Jason phoned Kat. "I'd like to see the kids," he begged.

Kat paused. "Well, you could come over for an hour in three weeks' time."

It was the longest three weeks of Jason's life, but at last the big day arrived. "I'm afraid they've gone to my parents," Kat sniggered.

"Come again in a month or so."

Tears welled up in Jason's eyes. How could his wife be so cruel? "It'll get worse," said Ed gloomily. "She'll bleed you dry through the CSA and then accuse you of being a paedophile. The police are already investigating me."

A month later a large envelope from the CSA arrived through the letterbox. "Give all your money to your wife," it said. "You count for nothing because you are a man."

A year had passed and Jason had scarcely seen his children. He decided to visit Ed. "I'm afraid he's committed suicide," said the policeman. "His wife drove him to it," Jason said angrily as his mobile started to ring. "I'm going to live in Newcastle," Kat laughed, "so you're going to see even less of the kids."

"Mummy's just bought a new plasma-screen TV and she makes us all go to a strange church," said Jake, when he called a year later. This was too much. The CSA were robbing him blind and now he, a God-fearing Tory who believed in family values, was powerless to prevent his children from being indoctrinated into a cult.

"I'm bored of the cult, so I'm marrying a librarian," Kat said two years later.

"Well, I'm marrying the dull Carol who's been hanging around for over five years," Jason snapped. "And we're moving next door to you." For the first time in 297 pages, a wry smile passed his lips.

The digested read ... digested

Widders dons her Batman suit

The Treehouse: Eccentric Wisdom from My Father on How to Live, Love and See

Naomi Wolf

Leonard Wolf, my father, is a tall, craggy bear of a man. He is a visionary poet who holds the secrets of the universe within his heart.

During a year of chaos after I turned 40, I bought a derelict house. Barren trees surrounded it, yet something inchoate had drawn me onwards. I sensed I was trying too hard as a writer, but something profound compelled me. I knelt in front of my father and begged him to teach me the 12 lessons of life. He smiled kindly. "Arise, grasshopper," he said. "Be still and listen." I waited for him to speak further, but the first lesson was over.

"Now you must use your imagination," Leonard said, drinking a yerba matte. I thought back to how he once bought me a tortilla-maker and decided to build my daughter, Rosa, a treehouse.

Lennie's childhood was fraught with violence and hardship, yet he remains the tenderest soul. "Destroy the box," he chanted. I thought about the prison I had created for myself, the high profile woman of letters. I needed to sublimate my ego, though obviously not to the extent of not writing about myself.

I was getting worried about my ability to teach my own students.

"Speak in your own voice," Leonard murmured, stroking his grey beard. "Find the voice of your child within."

I am your adoring Naomi

I'm going to write you poetwee

My friend Sophia was going through a tricky time in her marriage. Lennie wan Kenobi lay down his lightsabre. "Resist the power of the Dark Side," he spake, "and identify your heart's true desire."

Lennie is dressed like a '50s urban hipster as he hands over the notes for the sixth lesson. "Do everything with passion," he roars. Despite his womanising, which my mother and I forgive, he has always adored my mother and reaffirms his wedding vows daily.

I struggled to nail the railings to Rosa's treehouse. Leonard stepped into the garden. "Be disciplined with your gifts," he whispered. Blood flowed from his stigmata, as the nail went in.

Sophia had heeded Lennie's teachings and left her husband. Today she was bringing her new boyfriend Paul to stay with us. Paul ignored my children. Remembering the wisdom of the seventh lesson of *The Little Book of Calm*, I told her, "Pay attention to the details. He is not the chosen one." My father basked in Thoreauvian glory.

Lennie had been one of the original Bohemians, yet his work has never received the recognition of Kerouac and Ginsberg. "Your only wage is joy," he smiles beatifically. I nod. With this book, my career shall mirror his.

Some years ago, Leonard told us he had a son from a previous relationship. "Mistakes are part of the draft," he shrugged. I wept, for I had always sensed that part of my life was missing and now I felt complete.

The fall was coming and the treehouse is finished. As the light fades, Leonard's thoughts turn to endings. "Frame your work," he says, "for know ye that he who cannot die cannot live."

The world stood still. "I will not always be here," Leonard murmurs, his holy image flickering in the ether. "Sign it and let go." I howled with grief, then skipped with joy into the treehouse of renewal.

The digested read ... digested

I love my daddy

Acknowledgements

The longer the Digested Read goes on, the more I owe to others. So, many thanks are due to Lisa Darnell, Ben Siegle, Ruth Petrie, Michael Hann, Toby Manhire, Matt Keating, Felicity Lawrence, Leo Hickman, Ian Katz, Kath Viner, Will Woodward, Claire Phipps, Genevieve Carden, Paul Howlett, Paul Macinnes, Phil Daoust, Esther Addley, Amelia Hodsdon, Tim Lusher, Roger Rapoport, Richard Harris, Stephanie Calman and Nigel Wilcockson.